WRITTEN WITH THREE ANGELS IN MIND
Rest in Paradise:
Grandma Joann Cooper
Great Grandma Mildred Williams
Grandma Margaret Daniel

As I cast back the last few years of my life, I realize that…

I've won, just after losing

I've laughed, just after crying

I've identified true love, and then that of betrayal

I've felt powerful, and at times I'd weakened

I've endured confidence, after doubting myself

I've learned to trust, and experienced that of mistrust

I've learned to be kind, when other were unkind to me

I've tried to fit in, when I was meant to stand out

I've provided myself answers, just when I'd question

I've recognized true friendship, over that of the enemy

I've learned to be heroic, after believing I was my own villain

And through it all…

I've learned how to survive by acknowledging God's presence just after convincing myself that he was nowhere to be found

Ericka

Wise Words

Many of us hold on to our pain, afraid to reveal it. Ashamed to admit it. It is our duty to share what we know if it has helped us to move beyond some darkness in life.

-Iyanla Vanzant

What I know for sure is that speaking your truth is the most powerful tool we have.

-Oprah Winfrey

Don't depend too much on anyone in this world. Even your shadow leaves you when you're in darkness.

- Ibn Taymiyyah

Don't chase people. Be yourself, do your own thing and work hard. The right people-the ones who really belong in your life-will come to you. And Stay.

-Will Smith

ERICKA N. WILLIAMS

Contents

	My Confession	11
Preface:	Cooper + Daniel= Williams	19
1:	An Unsolved Mystery	23
2:	Beauty was her name	33
3:	Daddy is that you?	41
4:	A.T.L.	47
5:	Alone in a School so Cold	53
6:	Dear Sons: Mom Has Given Up	63
7:	Breaking the Law	67
8:	An Unplanned Plan	71
9:	There's No Place Like Home	81
10:	Shutting the Blinds	87
11:	Lost and Found	93
12:	I Do when I Really Don't	105
13:	Teac…HER	111
14:	Was it a M.A.T.C.H?	115
15:	July 13, 2017	119
16:	Desperately Seeking Strength	123
17:	Excuse Me As I Reminisce	127
18:	Empathy or Apathy	131
19:	I Call Her G Ma	137
20:	The Pill will Kill	141
21:	Recovery is a Craft	147
22:	The Devil is a Lie	151
23:	A Moment of Truth	155
24:	What I Lost in order to Win	157
25:	Obituary of Dead Words	161
26:	Dear Reader	163
27:	Forever Letters	165
	A Special Thank You	191

ERICKA N. WILLIAMS

My Confession

Some may consider me unreserved, and that is okay. Truth is, my story has been on my subconscious shelf for far too long and is in need of dusting off.

Coming to terms with burdensome times in my life is cathartic, as they have fashioned me into the woman I am today. There is no better way than to be truthful and confront what has retrained me for too long.

This is what I went through, this is who I am, and my aspiration is that someone can learn from me how to appreciate and understand the importance of overcoming, *as I have done*, and most importantly how to find salvation.

I have developed a deeper understanding of peace, and as I strive to live a joyous life, my desire is to rescue someone from internal discomfort particularly those who feel terribly alone. This is because many people I loved, *and I thought loved me*, walked out on me during some of my lowest points in life, leaving me to triumph on my own. And

I must admit it was agonizing. During those darkened moments, I was forced to armor myself with strength and shoo away my weaknesses. Furthermore, I redefined my self-worth, and made sure to honor God, who saved me from my loneliness and from myself *when I did not have a shoulder to lean on.* Not everyone is mighty enough to wrestle away despair and replace it with happiness. I was nearly too weak myself, but managed to triumph over.

    I know that there is someone somewhere who has grown tired of the canvas of his or her life being black. It's time to splash it with beautiful vibrant colors, maybe painting upon it stars, flowers, and many shades of happiness. I am officially committing my life to being God's servant, because through it all it was He who held me above water when I felt like drowning.

    This memoir has made it compelling for me to come face-to- face with critical conflicts that have slaughtered me emotionally. As I now reject those experiences that fail to harmonize my being. I have chosen to ward off excessive baggage in order to make the treks of my remaining days divine. For that reason, I consider my story authentic. So authentic, I chose to design my own front cover and polish my own pages. My desire is to share my story to the world, my way. *Never mind editing my book. It's time to edit my life.*

My prayer is that my story, journey, and lessons learned are testimonial and supportive to readers as they define their very best "*them*". I will no longer make myself the villain, and I hope the same for my audience. Much love.

Here is a story from one…

Bold Lady Inventing New Dreams Every Day

Psalm 119:133-136

Order my steps in thy word: and let not any iniquity have dominion over me. Deliver me from the oppression of man: so will I keep thy precepts. Make thy face to shine upon thy servant; and teach me thy statutes. Rivers of waters run down mine eyes, because they keep not thy law.

ERICKA N. WILLIAMS

BLINDED

FINDING FAITH AFTER LOSING SIGHT

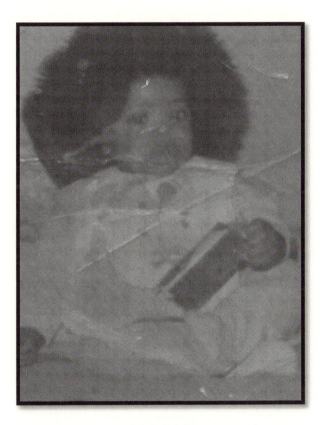

Little Ericka

ERICKA N. WILLIAMS

Preface

Cooper + Daniel = Williams

Emerging in life with *Williams* as a last name meant being at the end of the line. In elementary school, I was amongst the last call for a restroom break, so I often depended on cold water to wash away potty time germs because of there being no more soap. In middle school, ice cream after lunch for me meant settling for the picked over Giant Ice Cream Sandwich, or the partly melted Eskimo Pies because the Bubble Gum Snow Cones, Banana Fudge Bomb, and Strawberry Shortcakes were busily melting down my classmates fingers. In high school, I was nearly last to register for classes for the upcoming semester, so often missed the opportunity to land a spot on the class roster of those most sought out courses, *like Spanish*. I was forced to acquire a skill of reciting *bonjour* or *au revoir* when my interest was in *hola* and *adiós*. Even now as an adult, I am continually last. Of course, one might suppose that I have grown acclimated to gaining privilege just before the final call, but by no means have I accepted such bearings.

Ericka Williams is my name, *but* I was born to Donna Cooper and Leroy Daniel, my biological parents. Neither of which

My days as a toddler

legally bare the last name Williams. Neither of which experienced what it was like to *always* be last. Neither of which could even provide me with a valid reason for my unwelcoming position in line.

The complexities of my life dates back to December 1976, *just days before Rudolph was expected to chauffer Jolly Old Saint Nicholas* through the snowy skies of Cleveland, Ohio, *the city often referred to as the City of Lights*. I was born and so was my first burden. *It was as if we were Siamese twins.* That invader followed me into the real world, just on the other side of my mother's aching womb, much like a visibly clear shadow *trailing behind me just after my mom's last push*. It was as if it was breaking free from lonely darkness and in search for glaring lights Cleveland had grown widely known for, and I had become its companion.

That unwanted shadow of difficulties never seemed to subside. Instead it intensified, supplying more propane to already fumed moments of my life, becoming so agonizing I could only assume that my shadow was the first enemy I'd encountered; the demonic antagonist I couldn't break free from.

It had released itself from my mother's womb and leached on to my childhood and then eventually that of my adulthood, holding on near and dear much like that of paparazzi. From day one, my undesirable escort seemed to commence one hindrance after another; some I thought would kill me in due course.

During some of my most jinxed moments, I would find myself with an inquiring mind, wondering if it was because of my mother's faulty reputation of being regarded as the black sheep of the family. If there stood some validity, I'd conjured up in my mind that the curse was contagiously passed on to me instead of being cut with that of the umbilical cord, and not discarded as medical waste, much like that of the placenta.

At times, my developed life showed signs of being persecuted. As if my *evil twin* had taken hold to me like a disease; an epidemic that harmonized when I was at my most afflictive hours. Life as I knew it seemed to have been infected by what I believed to be a family curse. *I was blinded by evilness.*

Exodus 22:2-3

If a thief is found breaking in and is struck so that he dies, there shall be no bloodguilt for him, but if the sun has risen on him, there shall be bloodguilt for him. He shall surely pay. If he has nothing, then he shall be sold for his theft.

1

An Unsolved Mystery

As I reflect on throwback memories from my childhood, I now realize that life lessons for me, *after learning to articulate the alphabet*, were hustle and survival. And my mother's lifestyle required my involvement and provided me hands on experience.

H was for hustle, and S was for survival.

My father's life was no different, except it took *forever and a day* before his urge for a life in the fast lane would decelerate just enough to include me. He knew nothing of my existence, and I knew nothing of his. Over time though, discovered truth revealed to me that he was somewhere around twenty-four, and my mother was twenty-one when they made love, engaging in sexual reproduction. Only because it sounds a hell of a lot better than *f.u.c.k* or *s.c.r.e.w*, I'd much rather refer to their intimacy as making love. *But truth of their relationship was far-fetched.* I was *and am* the product of a casual one-nighter; an evening of freebase, rolled blunts, gin with a splash of orange juice, and a farewell abandoned by that of commitment or a promising future living with both mom and dad behind a picket fence.

My mother, often regarded as being the black sheep of the family, was cheated out of an opportunity to experience a full life with her own mother, my grandmother who I believed also suffered from that of a family curse. Joann was her name, but family and friends referred to her as Joe. Her last name was Cooper, *not Williams like mine*. Destruction of her life, perhaps set in motion by that of the curse, was plainly uniformed. *Alcohol was her foe*. It took nothing more to shatter her possibilities at experiencing a dazzling future.

Grandmother sitting on the porch

I might be slightly, *and I do mean slightly*, exaggerating when I say she consumed this addictive poison every day, *if not every other day*. Even though I spent a skimpy amount of time bonding with my grandmother, it is impossible for me to not remember how beautiful she was whenever sober.

Her hazelnut complexion shimmered evenly upon her from head to toe, emerging just below her thick glossy jheri curl. Her wide-set eyes were exceptionally large, complimenting her stunning smile, whenever she was privileged enough to expose a moment of happiness.

Those very same captivating eyes would often suffer a dramatic shift into a fireball blood shot red, making progress with growing darker *and darker* after every swallow of her chosen firewater.

Often times, she would relieve the weight of her difficult life by plopping down on her porch with a soft tune of B.B. King, or any of her favorite ole' school blues music, and sing and swig her way to a place of good spirits. The happiest she had ever been involved alcohol. Nothing else would dare compete with the joy she would receive from her spirit of choice, not even the birth of her daughter or her son, *who'd in time became a family mystery.* Delving into the intoxicant drink was her way of breaking free from her life of despair. *That of depression.*

I must admit that I was wet behind the ears during this time of my life, maybe somewhere around seven or eight. However my age was adequate enough to discern, *remembering until this day,* that once Joe reached that gleeful peak, a mystery companion would manifest and only she could make out his existence. *His name was Jody.* Whenever compelled to witness grandmother at the prime of intoxication, I would curiously stare her down as she talked to herself. *At least that is what I had thought.* From grandmother's perspective, Jody was right there seated next to her.

It was evident Jody gave grandmother butterflies. *She would giggle with him and sing sweet sounds to him. But then at some point in their interacting, that joy would transform into that of sorrowful tears.*

For Jody to be only a figment of imagination, he significantly influenced my grandmother's frame of mind. There were times that I would view her mixed emotions as being a bit comical, except for when she would boo-hoo her way into a siesta. And then there were times that I would inquire about her shift in emotions. I would ask about Jody, curious if he once existed and maybe met his dying day, or if he has only ever lived in my grandmother's mind. She would never convey the truth behind my inquiry, but after eavesdropping on her conversation with him a time or two, it was apparent that Jody was my grandmother's friendly ghost. Perhaps the enchanting groom she never had. Instead of being truthful to me about her imaginary romance, she would simply say, "*Don't worry about the snake in the grass. Worry about your own black ass.*" As one may imagine, I knew at that point it was time for me to depart from her presence.

I must confess, for a young girl like myself, her affairs were entertaining and hysterically funny. Fast forwarding to life as an adult, it causes me dire pain to even think of grandmother in those once witnessed circumstances. I wonder *if Jody had lived in the flesh,* what would be his attitude towards her massive consumption of a poison that would at times cause my grandmother to bare humiliation, particularly when she would urinate on herself, and sashay around with a sour smell of piss in her fifties. Then there would be those shameful moments of intoxication where she would walk down barely paved sidewalks, accented by shattered beer bottles, to the neighborhood convenience store to satisfy her craving for a Newport cigarette, *with no shoes upon her feet.*

If there really existed a curse, it wasn't that of a shadow. Instead, it was a riveting liquid, which knew its path quite well from that of grandmother's mouth to the seat of her pants, and at times upon a couch or loveseat.

Before reaching sixty, grandmother's life had been defeated by that of domineering alcoholism and cancer, its malicious ally.

Witnessing my grandmother live a favorable life remains a fantasy, as she is now resting in peace.

I must say, my mother has always been consumed with the desire to spend life with her mother without mortal reservations, and to have watched her wholeheartedly experience what society considers a productive life with a profession, a house made into a home, and a prince charmer who would have made her just as gleeful as Jody did by way of imagination.

* * *

As a teenager, grandmother had given birth to my mother, and to my uncle whom I've never met. My mother, until this very day, has never laid eyes on her brother, the sibling she'd always desired. His name was *or is* Anthony. God knows I wish I knew more, but his name is the beginning and end of my knowledge. No birthdate. No birth location. No nothing. *His life and its whereabouts remain a mystery, an unsolved detective story.*

Witnessing my mother, as she suffered from a heartache and heartbreak from curiosity of what life may have been like for him, caused me pain as well. I have always wished for a magic wand that would bring to life an answer to my mother's questioning if whether or not Anthony still walked in the flesh or had he at some point reunited with grandmother behind the golden gates of heaven.

Joe was too busy glorifying Jody to ever recount bona fide details that would produce that desirable brick road that lead to my uncle's whereabouts. For that reason, we will never have answers, and Anthony will never know his sister or her family. Sad to say, we will never know if he experienced living a harmonized life, *one accepted by society.*

My grandmother clutched on to my uncle's location and situations, taking the sacred truth deep down with her into the grave. And perhaps she is holding on to it tight within the palm of her hands, as she glorifies her days before God, because we have yet to receive a single clue. Her selfish decision once caused my mother to be nudged by one neighborhood rumor after another, all of which caused heartfelt twinges, as she hated to hear destructive possibilities about her brother.

I remember one day, I cautiously inquired about my uncle. Using passive discretion with this chitchatting about Anthony was a must because mom mourned evermore from just a simple thought of him. I was relieved to have practiced better judgment with my approach, because it seemed as if mom really wanted to share with me some of the heartfelt disclosures she had caught wind of, *nothing of concrete truth.* Mom could only spread to me the very rumor she had noted from local hearsay.

At one point, the gossip from undisclosed family members was that some daycare provider had abducted him right from the nursery one early morning, and was never captured. Before Joe's life had transitioned to the great beyond, she would irritably blurt out to my mother, "Dammit, he died." This response would transpire subsequently after mom's decision to barge in on grandmother and Jody's rendezvousing. Mother wanted to believe, *deep down in her heart,* that death was not the answer. But she was mature enough to know that a drunken mind speaks a sober heart. By just the thought, my mother would weep tears of despair.

It was as if mother stood on one's own, on a deserted island, confined by an ocean that had taken on her burden. Then by relieving her stress by washing to shore answers, particularly a map leading to Anthony's long lost whereabouts. Since the thought was just a fantasy, it would have been great for mother to have a trusting, heartfelt family member she could turn to for comforting or her desired remedy, but even that was a fiasco.

This was no laughing matter to mother, but that didn't stop the heart-wrenching witticism she would endure from those she loved. For example, "You need to let sleeping dogs lie dead." My uncle's position in life haunted my mother. Her consistent inquiries never meant to stir things up or cause difficulties for anyone. It just wasn't an easy mission for her to let an unanswered past perish. But the end result of her detective efforts meant accepting that she would mope into her adult life suffering from never finding out the truth. My prayer is that mother has the opportunity to hug Anthony and to tell him that she loves him. Nevertheless, this pain lives with her to this very day.

Mommy experienced life blinded by hope.

Colossians 1:26-27

"The mystery which has been hidden from ages and from generations, but now has been revealed to His saints. To them God willed to make known what are the riches of the glory of this mystery among the Gentiles; which is Christ in you, the hope of glory."

ERICKA N. WILLIAMS

2
Beauty was her Name

My mother's picture perfect beauty often served as the trailblazer to opportunities, some good and some not so good. Drifting through life motherless and fatherless often made hiding under a rock seem to be the perfect escape from her loneliness, but she knew that wasn't clever thinking. From the aid of her attractiveness, mommy often found herself landing on a path of landmines, *exploding one after another.* Like her brother she never knew her father, so some family members diligently tried to protect her from street life eruptions. It was rumored that my grandfather was anything

Mommy during her teen years

but black, and it was obvious from mommy's heavenly honey complexion. *In my eyes*, my mother's beauty is like no other. Perhaps I would have a deeper understanding of the root of her attractiveness had I met her grandmother, my *great-grandmother*. Many times, I had heard that she was considered to be a black Marilyn Monroe beauty. If that were the case, she was indeed beautiful because that actress was stunning.

My mother found great joy in sharing with me how she often gazed at her grandmother's *eye-appeal* before she succumbed to cancer, *just as Joe did*. Mommy was at the tender age of twelve-years old when her grandmother transitioned the way of all flesh. *Her name was Mildred.*

I still believed there existed a family curse, and it had made its way from the beginning to the ending of Mildred's being. Next it had scribbled its way into Joann's life until erasing her from the living, all of this before planting a seed in my mother's life.

Mother's eye-appeal gravitated to those in the streets. As a result, she was introduced to a white powder often fired through a crack pipe. *I remember she used to refer to that pipe as a glass D.I.C.K.* This blaze fulfilled her desire to feel good, which was her ultimate mission. I had heard each puff of the pipe would send tingles up and down her body, and that is what made it addicting. Another hit would have to follow just to avoid the comedown of the stimulation.

Accepting this as recreational living provided mommy with an escape from family members poking fun at her for being the offspring of a dysfunctional home. Because my beautiful mother always desired that of a family, much like what she would often envy of others, she considered it necessary to initiate developing a family with street thugs who, *in most cases*, worshipped the ground she walked on. They treated her with a special type of loyalty, and so in her eyes they had become her extended family. It was cocaine that kept them united. Her moral compass had led her to being referred to as an aunt by some and a sister by others. This made her feel cared for, desired, appreciated, and most importantly, *loved*.

Perhaps cocaine was a spawn from the probable family curse, because it caused mommy significant distractions throughout life *until many years later*.

As a matter of fact, it was cocaine that victimized mommy into becoming a subject of robbery by someone she had perceived to be a trusting friend. This cocaine addict left her high in dry in howling wind, and piling snow that *blinded* the night with white dust, much like that within the crack pipe. He stripped her of a posh mink coat, just after snatching her purse from around her wrist. *These items were destined to become a pawn for a hit.* It was cocaine that also guided my mother in the direction of being an eyewitness to a convenient store robbery, *by one of her goon family members*, who also bared the obsession with cocaine. Distraught by what she had witnessed, mommy was left with no option but to declare her innocence *and protect her freedom*. So this meant being a snitch. She cared less about the old school cliché' *snitches get stitches* because her freedom was in jeopardy. Because of this, without hesitation she chose to cooperate with law enforcement to rid this dope head from the streets.

It's a good thing I was too young to truly make sense of the struggles my mother faced. Furthermore, I am forever grateful that she made the decision to wait until I had become an adult to inform me of how another dope head family member desired to stroke the center of my thighs. His desire was to climb his maturity on top of me and widen the dimensions of my vagina. He wanted to bury my virginity away for life by jabbing his mature penis into me, a naïve little girl. Even now as an adult, I am clueless as to who this individual is, but I am confident in saying this sexual predator is thankful for life, because my mother depended on her street family to assure that he would forever regret his desire to fondle a young girl who hadn't even endured true puberty. Mother nature hadn't even begun to punch the monthly clock with me. If there in deed existed a family curse, it did not conquer its objective.

My mother's attractiveness not only withheld the attention of street thugs, *some of which were cross-dressing boosters*. Her eye-appeal had exposed her to the life of the rich and famous, *although she wasn't rich or famous*. In fact, I'd learned over the years that I nearly had a brother or sister by one of Cleveland Brown's muscular playmakers. An abortion intercepted the possibilities of this child walking a single mile in my shoes. *Perhaps this baby escaped that of the family curse.*

Mommy was content with having one child, but I had always yearned for a sister or brother. My fantasy with having a sibling was not a part of mommy's plan. I knew this because she often shared with me how she underwent two abortions and one miscarriage prior to pregnancy with me, which often led to jokes that my distinct personality was simply a combination of her terminated pregnancies. She had no interest in birthing another.

Her exposure to the rich and famous included attracting and dating a member of a soul music vocal group from Detroit,

Michigan, as well as a member of one of the most popular Philadelphia soul groups of the 1970s.

One I vaguely remember was a member of a funk band that popularly exploded in the early 1980s. Even today, I find myself boogying to the beat of some of her sidekicks. It's no surprise that my mother would attract such an audience, with her two-shade or mixed beauty.

Her mimicked life of the rich and famous was plagued by not just cocaine, *but alcohol too.*

Mommy was a mean and evil drinker. She was so unpleasant while under the influence, that friends appointed the name of her alter ego as Sybil, a psychiatric patient whose life had been portrayed in the 1970s. I am willing to bet that those individuals who witnessed mommy's acting would agree that *she missed her calling*, because she played the hell out of woman with multiple personalities. After a couple of vodka and cokes chilled with an ice cube or two, mommy would find interest in swinging from that of the dining room chandelier, or portraying Patti Labelle by kicking her shoes off of her feet, landing them clean across the room. As I reflect on my mother's role as Sybil, I can't help but remember some of her theatrical occasions.

Yes, mommy had her fair share of dating celebrities here and there, but her bank account significantly benefited from that of sugar daddies. She knew how to *cake them* as the saying goes. No matter the occasion, Donna and Sybil were flirtatious, sweet, and charming. There was this one tall fairly slim man with a well-managed afro. He walked her straight into a local new car dealership and negotiated his way into a car loan just for mommy, *exchanging his signature for the keys to a spanking new Toyota Camry*. His kind gesture also included keeping her equipped with *pocket change*. As I matured over the years, I would wonder the rationale behind his actions. As it turns out, mommy suckered him into believing she was months away from being visited by that of a stork. She fooled him real good; especially after using money he'd given her to purchase a fake tie on pregnancy belly from a costume store *only to be worn in his presence*. Mom would demand that I stay quiet, especially because I knew that as soon as she would send him on his way, she would be back to her size four or six in the waist. *I was still the only child, and that was not going to change.*

At a very young age, my mother proved to be talented. Therefore, I sometimes wonder what life may have been like for her had she not suffered from that of a dual personality brought on by drugs and alcoholism. *Without a doubt she could have inked some Hollywood gigs.* Having experienced a life of hustle and bustle with my mom was no easy venture, and as I matured over time, I would pray for the day my mother would choose to get high on life, instead of that of what a glass pipe had to offer. *It would be years later that my blessing would blossom into fruition.* During my intimate moments with God, I would also ask him to cast away the family curse so that it would no longer taunt her. What I failed to pray was that the family curse I believed existed would bypass my life, but instead it eventually seemed that it was preparing to aggressively escort me through my journey, one step at a time. *I was blinded by hallucination.*

Mommy and Me

Ephesians 6:11

"Put on the whole armor of God, that you may be able to stand against the schemes of the devil."

Three

Daddy, *is that you?*

In the fullness of time, we met face-to-face. He was tall, dark, and handsome. His features were defined in a way that would dare alert a passerby of his delinquent acts.

His presence excited me, causing my eyes to leak with tears. Although my vision slightly blurred, I was able to distinguish a bit of myself in him. *Particularly in his brown eyes*. They were wide and alert, just like mine.

Little attention was paid to the gift he nestled under his arm. Although in my quick glimpse, I did notice that it was a Cabbage Patch doll, *my favorite*.

For the first time, I was able to say just what I had yearned for so many years.

"Hi daddy."

There was no need for one to ask about my day at school because the excitement was tatted to my face, a joyful moment I was able to gloat in front of my classmates.

For many nights I would lay awake, watching the time trickle down, marking another minute *wondering about my daddy*. Finally having experienced it, I couldn't tell if my time with him was genuine or simply a blessing in disguise. Either way, this was my opportunity to showcase my parents, *both mommy and daddy.*

Together they stood before me in the congested cafeteria, as if we were one happy family. Voices and footfalls from my classmates were earsplitting, yet it was busy silence to me because I heard nothing but daddy's voice as he said *hello* to me for the first time in my entire life.

Daddy was having lunch with me.

This was a big deal for elementary aged students like myself.

This picture was taken long before meeting daddy

Before this day, I was on the outside looking in watching classmates scurry into their parent's arms in the course of those surprise visits during lunchtime. I was a bit envious from witnessing how fortunate they were to have the opportunity to bypass a lunch that robbed the joy of eating. A typical lunch would include chocolate milk secured in a plastic bag, served with a dry burger, which was stacked between a rock hard bun. Often times, some toy and a golden arch accompanied their midday meal. Mommy was a single mother, so I would have to wait until after school to have a kid's meal.

If I had my way, I would have experienced that joy time and time again. I was paralyzed with happiness. I felt protected, as most daughters do in their daddy's arms. At the same time, I suffered with internal trembles, afraid that the moment would never present itself again.

I was right.

My first time having lunch with daddy was also my last. Perceiving this as a blessing was unattainable. Instead, it was luck, and now I was emotionally conflicted.

Daddy while in penitentiary

* * *

Daddy was a *dope pusher, drug addict,* and all around *scandalous felon.* His very first encounter with being stoned was from glue. I am not quite sure if it was the liquid glue or the glue stick. Either way, he took pleasure in getting a whiff of it, never mind using it to fulfill a school project. The thrill he would experience stimulated his childhood. But eventually his immune system would laugh at the intent of the glue to rouse him, so he turned to marijuana and nose candy.

Daddy was also a robber, mugger, sneak thief. In 1967, he surrendered five years of freedom for a measly sixty dollars. Not six hundred dollars or six thousand dollars. *Sixty.* His scheme to disguise himself as a commuter, in order to rob a local city transit bus, did not quite go as planned. His decision to execute such an act landed him slam in the state penitentiary, where he would spend his remaining teenaged years. With that said, his high school diploma read *state penitentiary,* since he completed his academic work behind bars. I am confident that his experience is what defines that of *school of the hard knocks.* During his time out of reach from society, I guess it's appropriate to say he was productive, as much as one can be without the luxury of freedom.

Aside from graduating from high school while incarcerated, daddy exhibited his talents with being the offensive leader on their football team. He had earned his teammate's confidence by being an assertive quarterback. After the ending of their football season, daddy served as a firefighter for the correctional facility, responsible for putting out fires for others, since he couldn't figure out how to extinguish the flames of his own life.

Daddy also exhibited his unruly qualities. So he tolerated many days of solitary confinement, eating nothing but slices of dry bread for breakfast, lunch, and dinner. All of this was because of his aggressive temper and abrupt swiftness to engage in physical altercations. Punishment for him meant no freedom, no more football, no mayonnaise, or even a piece of bologna.

Daddy's time in captivity served as an inadequate sanction because the moment he stood beneath the sunny skies, he was back to his immoral behavior. Over and over again, he would land under lock and key as if he was simply playing a game of Monopoly and held in possession a pyramid of *get out of jail free* cards to protect him from the misery of being sent up the river. Imprisonment had become his norm.

Some acts were misdemeanors.

Some acts were felonies.

One of his charges was for homicide. But by the grace of God, he was found *not guilty* of robbing one of *his or her* life. If the results had differed, I would have to wonder if it would have been beneficial for me to be abandoned by daddy, as opposed to having a reputation of having a father who was a murderer.

Still he continued with criminal acts. It was evident that incarceration did not faze daddy because if it had, I would like to believe that he would have committed himself to being a positive citizen *instead of a culprit.*

After learning of daddy's ruthless cold-hearted commitment to the streets, I could not help but question *if he too was the black sheep of the family.* I wondered. If this were the case, I stood no chance. **Daddy was blinded by foolishness.**

Psalm 146:9

The LORD protects the strangers; He supports the fatherless and the widow, But He thwarts the way of the wicked.

4

A.T.L.

Ohio, Texas, Florida, and Georgia were all considered home at one point in my life *before reaching the eighth grade*. Bystanders could have easily presumed that mommy and I were ducking and dodging the law or that I was some military young'un, as much as we loaded and unloaded U-Hauls. Neither were the case, but I am willing to bet that we migrated from one state to the next more than some of those respected service men and women who traveled, sacrificing their lives, while defending America the beautiful.

Oftentimes, our residential shifts were prompt. They were so unforeseen that on an ordinary morning I would drag my feet off the bed, rub my knuckles onto my eyes just before showering and taming the morning shock of my hair by shoving it into a rubber band. Then I would make my way to school, only to return to packed and stacked cardboard boxes. They would be lined against bare walls and bursting at the rims, yet taped from one side to the next ready to be loaded to the U-haul and transported to what would become our next address. *The only advantage to this transformation was that I would not have to shuffle through my notebooks in search for that night's homework assignments.* I took pleasure in referring to this as my homework free pass. Instead, I would dump the clutter into the trashcan and prepare my backpack for a new school and new disarray that would blossom within the confinement of the zipper.

During my years of traveling with mommy

Mommy and I were frequent flyers on wheels, and I could never get use to the grime and sweat stench that traveled with us inside of the rental trucks. They all shared the same aroma, except for those that hauled chain smokers. In that case, the lingering smell of nicotine would take a seat on my lap, and partake in the discomfort of my seatbelt. Another thing, there existed the displeasure of the bumpiness from what felt like worn threads around the tires. The misery of this is what introduced me to my lifelong suffering of motion sickness, *but that's another story.*

Anyways, mom wasn't shy of change, so this was the rationale behind our frequent relocating.

The sudden changes only caused me to become terribly ignorant when it comes to childhood discussions. As a matter of fact, I make every effort to avoid them at all cost because I am clueless when it comes to remembering the names of the elementary schools I've attended, *something meant to be uncomplicated.* I am oblivious when it comes to remembering that teacher who terrified me, or my favorite if I ever had one at some point in my younger days. Friends…I had them, but can't remember a single name. Not one. As trendy as social media is nowadays, and how confident I am that some old childhood friends would be active members and maybe even mutual friends to some, I cannot even recollect a nickname to use as a starting point in locating them. Those memories are vague. The echelon of knowledge I have of my primary years in school is much like the wisdom I have of the uncle I have never laid eyes on. Eventually Atlanta, Georgia would be where the U-Haul would stop for me though.

* * *

Establishing a stable lifestyle was finally becoming reality, as mommy and I became *Georgia Peaches* settling on red clay, the distinct color of most of the state's soil.

The culture of Atlanta differed considerably from other cities. I realized this after hearing others refer to it as *Black Mecca*. Of course, other cities once considered home by mommy and me had a decent amount of well off blacks, but nothing like A.T.L.

Black prosperity was everywhere, *in every zip code*. Not just those areas that lacked high-performing schools. *Particularly those areas stereotypically known for the swirl of drugs and violence by young black men, or single women having babies.*

Success was everywhere.

Doctors, attorneys, and civil rights activist…you name it.

They were everywhere. And the older I'd become the more fascinating I found this to be.

The four zero four area code eventually became known as the *Empire City of the South* for more reasons than just the brave accomplishments of Dr. Martin Luther King Jr., one of few black activists I'd learned about prior to our relocating to his birthplace.

Life in the south offered me the opportunity to gain knowledge of other renowned historians, *like Alonzo Herndon*, one of Atlanta's first millionaires, whose mansion accented the nearby Atlanta University Center. And then there was Auburn Avenue, a historic district slam in the heart of Atlanta. And the street that embraced more black history than I could ever specify.

I will never fail to remember the day I learned about Auburn Avenue's contribution to the African American race. It was during my years as a college student attending Clark Atlanta University, one of ATL's historically black colleges. Dr. Jenkins, one of my professors *who would never smile*, required the class to develop a city documentary by way of photography. It was this very assignment that revealed to me this cultural center of black history.

During my visit, an aggressive panhandler approached me. My initial instinct was to shoo him away, but his expertness of this avenue was just what I needed to attain my desirable passing grade for this class. So as we drifted further away from my car, he would make a point of teaching me of the once eminent black-owned businesses, entertainment venues, churches and even Hanley Bell Street Funeral Home, which is where Dr. King's family assembled on the day of his homecoming celebration.

Our trek lasted longer than I desired, and to this day I am grateful for the destitute gentleman. His intelligence confirmed to me that brainpower at times considered filthy dirt streets a pillow at night, or a condemned house as roof over their head, even on a thundery night. *Intellect lived in Atlanta, and it thrilled me to call it home.* ***I was blinded by possibilities.***

Matthew 7:1-2

Do not judge, or you too will be judged. For in the same way you judge others, you will be judged, and with the measure you use, it will be measured to you.

5

Alone in a School So Cold

By the time I had reached sweet sixteen and sophomore status in high school, I'd accomplished more than most girls in my age bracket. I had acquired the ability to gap my legs wide opened to the words *I love you*, given birth to two children *by two different guys*, and depended on hardworking tax-payers to contribute to the government so that I could afford groceries. *Food stamps.* I had even been jailed one time for simple battery. A quarrel between mommy and me landed me my first *and last* encounter with handcuffs, which I quickly considered an unappealing accessory around my wrist. I remember suffering from the sharpness of them as they jabbed into my skin, scraping me down to my flesh. I was scared, so paid little attention to the blood that slithered from the slash. *They definitely weren't my ideal bangles.*

In spite of our mother-daughter feud, mommy had attempted everything short of dropping to her knees while begging the police officer to have mercy on me by not locking my arms behind my back with those things. The officer gave less than a damn that I was a terrified sixteen-year-old little girl. In her eyes, a law was just that, *a law*, and I was going to be treated no differently from that of a sixty-year-old man who had just beaten his wife.

"I am required to handcuff you," the officer blurted just before directing me into the backseat of her patrol car.

*Let me say this again…*HER patrol car.

There existed no comfort to this ride. The plastic seats were rock hard; I guess to eliminate the possibility of violent arrestees ripping them to shreds. It was evident that the previous jailbird to be chauffeured before me was drunk enough to treat the very seat I sat on as a urinal. *I felt like a criminal.*

* * *

There around me was nothing but deep-set cubes of concrete, and no windows for me to see how much time had passed. I would have given anything to know if the happy sun still shined or if I sat underneath the shy moon. The path of my daddy's life was becoming my very own. The only difference between he and I is, it only took one time for me to learn to avoid going back by any means. Time spent in solitude made me wonder how one could frequent a place that smelled of blood, sweat, and tears, and I was certain daddy wanted to see me be better than he was with making life decisions.

My rebellious behaviors led me to eviction from my mother's house. "Two bitches can't live under the same roof," she yelled just before showing me the door, as if I didn't already know my way to it. The very moment I stood before the outside world as a mother to two children, I felt as if I stood on unfamiliar grounds. Things seemed foreign. And I didn't know if I should go right or left in search for direction.

During my high school days

Just as I thought I'd discovered the sweetness of a busted cherry, my relationship with mommy had grown sour. It wasn't long that I would learn that the cherry young girls my age were often curious about wasn't exactly sugared in any way. In fact, after time it proved to be very dry.

I still believed it was that of a curse, and it was horny for graving my family just as I was for being grown before my time. It had encroached on the privacy of Mildred's life, tormenting her until her dying day. It had become the chaser to grandmother's beer, liquor, or wine, prompting her to alcoholically drown herself in pure misery. It had disguised itself as something or someone who loved my mother, leading her to believe that the street life was by far the greatest accomplishment she could achieve. It blinded my father of his parenting responsibilities and motivated him to stray away from his precious daughter. And now it was leading me to believe that everything touched by me would turn to stone.

* * *

My high school experience was completely opposite from that of most of my classmates. *I was the decision maker.* I was in control of my bedtime, what I would have for dinner, and if I wanted to go to school on any given day. Not only had I been evicted from living with my mom, she had since packed up the U-Haul again and headed for the west coast, leaving me to fend for myself in ATL.

My classmates depended on the wellbeing of their lifestyle from that of *at least* one parent. As they would participate in after school activities and await the arrival of their parents to chauffeur them home, I would *time* watch just to make sure I'd arrived in time to pick up my own children from childcare *before being charged a late fee.*

Extracurricular activities provided my schoolmates the opportunity to participate in band, chorus, cheerleading, or some other after school interest. *I wanted the same life.* Becoming a successful high school swimmer was my desire. I wanted to contribute my rhythmic strokes to that of our winning team. Unfortunately, there would be no gliding like a dolphin for me. Instead of diving into the deep end of an eight-foot deep swimming pool, I had to figure out how to survive the whirlwind of my destructive life path.

Those I once shared kindred spirits with had turned their deaf ear to me,

Pregnant with my first child

disregarding whatever qualities *I possessed at being a friend.* All in all, I had become just what most of their parents had hoped to safeguard them from. *Teenaged parenting.* To the eyes of the beholder I was bad influence. *Sixteen, with a mug shot,* and *two children* meant I couldn't be a good friend *I guess.* Nevertheless, much like my mother once experienced, my classmates patronized me, only causing me to suffer from rumors they would stir-up.

    Ericka doesn't know who her baby fathers are.

    Ericka is pregnant a third time.

    Ericka…Ericka…Ericka

    It was a frequent thing for me to transition from one classroom to the next while forced to make my way by pointing fingers and whispers accompanied by chuckles of my undesirable accomplishments. This is when I would remind myself that *sticks and stones may break my bones, but words would never hurt me,* as the long-lived cliché goes. It was those very words that shielded me from underestimating myself even more than I had already done. *At times it was easier for me to criticize myself rather than believe in myself.* That good ole' cliché couldn't always help me, though. One time in particular was when my name was a candidate on the senior class superlatives list. It was that point in time that I would endure sure suffering.

    Ericka Williams: Most likely to have a lot of kids.

Luckily, there was a difference between those literal superlatives and those considered satirical. I was thankful that my name was only used for mocking purposes, and not the intent of posing humiliation on a page of the class of 1995 yearbook.

Senior class picture

Even still I was damaged emotionally.

Sad to say, some of those who voted for such foolishness were at one point considered a friend before I'd become a mother.

I was ashamed.

I was embarrassed.

I was struggling academically.

I was fearful that I would fail at experiencing what it was like to be a high school graduate.

One negative thought after another, I was growing *confident* in my *lack of confidence*.

This time of my life was all about conquering negative thoughts.

Dropout Ericka said Lucifer as he set on my left shoulder.

Believe Ericka, said Jehovah on my right.

Graduating from high school no longer seemed to be a practical goal for me. Instead it withered into an unattainable dream, and I was afraid I'd never achieve it. A couple of my classmates had become teen moms and had dropped out. *What made me believe I was different*? Now I was not only the joke of the family, as aunts and cousins would whisper gibberish, such as *"Ericka is going to drop out of high school and work two minimum wage jobs."*

Sure enough those around me, including my unwanted companion *the shadow I could not escape*, tormented me. My internal conflicts were also the antagonists defeating the hero I once believed I could be when it came to rescuing me from that of failure.

Nevertheless, I stood steadfast in my decision to keep my head up, as I eluded one rumor after another, allowing only my tears to stroll downward as I dragged myself from one class to the next in search for my high school diploma. ***I was blinded by possibilities.***

Deuteronomy 31:6

"Be strong and courageous. Do not be afraid or terrified because of them, for the L ORD your God goes with you; he will never leave you nor forsake you."

6

Dear Sons: Mom Has Given Up

FEAR is a controlling word. *One that often suffocated me as if it were invisible hands.* It was corroding the person God meant for me to be. *Decisions I had made in my life taught me this.* Those four letters orchestrated my decision to abandon my two sons, leaving them with their fathers, grandmothers, uncles and aunts…*any family member willing to take care for them.* Brothers with the same mother were stripped of the opportunity to live under the same roof. They were cheated of the chances to share secrets, have pillow fights, sibling rivalries, quarrels, or the making of memories period. Fear was my assailant, and it had caused me to rob my children of these opportunities *like a thief in the night.* They were innocent little boys, and I was a blameworthy mother.

I dare not to seek justification for believing my decision was right, nor will I ever be able to apologize enough to them. There is no excuse great enough to suffice my decision to forfeit responsibilities as their mother, but at *seventeen and alone,* my life had already become unbearably grueling. *And I was cowardly afraid.* They deserved stability, and I was incapable of supplying this necessity, therefore it seemed to be the right thing to do. *I could think of no other option.* Still, that does not make it right, so I will forever live with an incurable gash to my heart.

Truth be told, I never considered the course of actions that would follow me for years to come *much like the family curse I believed existed.*

* * *

Before relinquishing my parental responsibilities, the three of us depended on others to sustain. It was a good thing both of my sons were from fathers who had families with a sacred bond, *and a heart.* Because after my mother dismissed me from living in her house, it was one of my son's grandmothers who graciously opened her home to my family of three. Her name was Millie. Time there was *uncomfortably* comfortable. She spared her guest room to me, and provided a filling meal every day, but I could never consider it home. She extended her hospitality to me while others allowed *the doorknob to hit me where the good Lord split me.* This, as one may imagine, was an overwhelming emotional period in my life, filled with fear, pain, sadness, and a series of bad decisions. *As time passed, I had become more of a dependent of welfare, instead of one who contributed to the success of Black Mecca, as I once desired.*

Isaiah 41:10

"Fear not, for I am with you; be not dismayed, for I am your God; I will strengthen you, I will help you, I will uphold you with my righteous right hand."

ERICKA N. WILLIAMS

7

Breaking the Law

Child abandonment was against the law. I learned this after becoming a defendant in child support court. *I had broken the law,* and my youngest son's father, the plaintiff, was going to make me pay for it *literally.* According to the law, I had deserted my responsibilities to provide care for my children. I failed to care for their physical health, and I failed at protecting them. I failed at providing for them all together. My wrongdoings made me a culprit of the court system for the second time. *This time without handcuffs.*

I remember surveying the courtroom as I awaited the legal proceeding of my case. Other young mothers too occupied seats upon the parallel wooden benches, but they were positioned on the left side of the room near my plaintiff, as I sat as the only young mother on the right surrounded by their defendants, some of which considered dead beat dads just as I had convinced myself of being a deadbeat mom. Unlike myself, these ladies were the payees of child support, and I was a *judge ruling* away from being the payer.

I was a young student committed to working fifteen hours per week, *if that,* at a local retail store, so surely the judge would bare sympathy for me, right? *Wrong.* The decision maker cared less about my instability, or my part time work status. He still pounded that gavel against a block of wood before sending me on my way, right out the courtroom with a hefty bill of three hundred and twenty dollars per month *made payable to my baby daddy.*

My second son during a visit

The outcome of this case defined to me the true meaning of friendship betrayal. It was because of my "baby daddy's relationship with someone I once viewed as being a best friend that I would scramble to pay to him this court ordered invoice. *No more of doing what I could when I*

My oldest son during a visit

could. Sexual encounters he had shared with someone I valued as being a confidant resulted in him not only parenting a second child, but also warming the very seat I sat in awaiting the judge. She had become the plaintiff and he her defendant. Of course the outcome of his case was child support, and l had to help replenish his monthly payout to her. *At least some of it.* I had heard he was ordered to pay more than my three hundred and twenty dollars. Even still, I replaced some of it.

He made sure that I knew this too, as I scurried my way past him towards the courtroom exit doors.

"She was your friend, so split that bill with me," *he laughed as I held on tight to my feeling of humiliation.* Like many times before, I wondered if this was the work of a family curse because at this point, I was left wondering if there really existed a God. If so, I needed him. ***I was blinded by chief evil spirits.***

John 1:9
"If we confess our sins, he is faithful and just to forgive us our sins and to cleanse us from all unrighteousness."

8

An Unplanned Plan

No one ever *schooled* me on the relevance of planning my future, preparing for a college career, and managing or overcoming debt accrued from student loans. I had to make sense of these things on my own *by way of trial and error.*

In 1998 I applied, gained acceptance and began my college career at Clark Atlanta University, a historically black college centrally located in the heart of Atlanta. A college considered a private school, a college with a mighty price tag, *far too expensive for a student of my caliber*, but the only college to accept me as a less than B, *and at times a less than C,* average student.

I'd applied to become a student with Georgia State, but was denied the opportunity to gain a collegiate experience with the university. I even took a chance at applying to The University of Georgia, but knew deep down in my heart that I was only fooling myself by doing so. I still took the chance at being a candidate of the required affirmative action acceptances. Even still, I am certain that some admission office assistant practiced their slam-dunk techniques with my application, and transcripts right into the nearest wastebasket. I knew my credibility lacked the requirements of Bulldog Nation, the largest college in Georgia. *It didn't hurt me to try.*

Without a career in mind, I celebrated my acceptance to CAU because I believed this was my opportunity to become a better *me*.

During those moments of trying to find myself

My career as a collegiate student began without a declared major. Even still I was a college student. This was my opportunity to share a commonality with my high school classmates, some of which attended the same college. This was also my opportunity to throw a monkey wrench into the future others had established for me. Speculations were that I would be a high school dropout and settle for working not one *but two* minimum waged jobs. I was determined to prove them wrong *as I had done by graduating from high school,* although I did accept one minimum wage job flipping chargrilled burgers before topping them with lettuce and tomato, and adding a side of fries.

Most importantly, I wanted to prove myself right for believing that I could establish a foundation for myself, one that would make life better for my children and me.

Discontinuing my high school career was never an implemented plan, *but it had been contemplated*. Self-dignity saw to it that I would become a high school graduate, even if it meant meeting the minimum high school requirements. With my two sons in the audience, I proudly received my "general" high school diploma; at the same time others received academic or advanced academic acknowledgements. This experience was hailed as a milestone for me, as I remember there were other teen moms in school with me who forfeited their opportunity to wear a cap and gown. This aspect of my life awarded me the opportunity to feel accomplished. But then I was reminded that…I was not making the grade with parenting my two sons. *What I believed to be the family curse continued to gain advantages over my life.*

Embarking on a new phase of my life without them burdened me. And I know they were afflicted by my poor judgment as their mother. As the weekend parent, Sunday night drop-offs were emotionally excruciating.

I felt shamed, and rightfully so as they would cry their way out of my arms and into the arms of those who picked up my slack. It was the rearview mirror of my car that would smack me with guilt, as I would watch them wail to others as I drifted further away from their presence. God forbid those occasions they would signal to me a farewell with their precious hands.

The babies, who lived within the boundaries of my womb for nine months, were no longer able to synch their heartbeats with mine. My babies had to tell their mom goodbye, as I drove off in search for myself.

* * *

Finally, I'd declared journalism as my major. I wanted to be a journalist. I was going to witness real live events and write articles about them as a reporter. I was going to have a real-live career that would take care of my children, *and my child support responsibilities*. I had psyched myself up to be thrilled about my decision. But truth is, my decision to conduct interviews was ultimately the decision of my first collegiate friend. *Her name was Camille.* This was her major, so I followed her lead. Both of us pursing the same major meant parallel classes. I guess this made me a naïve follower, but I didn't know any better.

* * *

After five years, sixty thousand dollars of college debt, and now baby number three on the way, I wore a cap and gown for the second time. *This time as a college graduate.* I'd used my declared major just enough to establish a zeal for photography, examine the lives of local individuals, acquire student loan collection calls, and to meet my now third baby father. *This was the gist of it.*

Recent college graduate and pregnant with third son

Taking a look back at this moment in my life, I would have to say that I was distracted from self-destruction brewing just for me. After all, I was on my way towards becoming the first in my immediate family to gain a college degree. If there existed a family curse, it was being defeated. Truth is, the curse I believed existed had only spoon-fed me an appetite. I'd yet to experience the main course. ***I was blinded by truth.***

Proverbs 3:5-6

Trust in the Lord with all your heart and lean not on your own understanding; in all your ways submit to Him, and He will make your paths straight.

AND THEN THERE WERE THREE

My three boys and me

MY LITTLE FAMILY YEARS LATER

Photo courtesy of photopeople.com

ERICKA N. WILLIAMS

9

There's No Place Like Home

Every day the sweet-tart smell of balsamic vinegar and Parmesan cheese would welcome me home from a long workday. And although that aroma may have stemmed from that of my son's armpits, or the dirty socks ejected from their sneakers left at the front door *and not from a blend of ingredients atop my stove*, I found this odor gratifying. The sudden whiff of it evoked a feel of contentment, causing me to rejoice now that my two oldest sons were permanently home with their little brother and me. An earshot

With my boys at the neighborhood festival

of them calling out for *mommy* was sweet sounds, at least for the first few years. We were living on the same turf and no longer that of divided territory.

At times I would celebrate their success from passing a quiz or test *after an exhausting night of studying*. Or because of being proactive with tackling their chore list by washing dishes, *including those stashed away under their beds*, which had become a horrifying science project for lack of better words. Partaking in good times with my boys was a significant deed in our house, but no longer could they look to me as the fun weekend parent. If they failed to meet the expectations of their teachers, there were consequences to pay.

My heart was committed to seeing to it that they'd experience a favorable outcome in elementary all the way to their last high school assignment, no matter their least favored subjects. It was a good thing I took advantage of lunchtime surprises with them while they were required to walk in single file lines because soon after they were gifted freedom as older students, I swear it seemed to be an imaginary sign plastered on their school's front door reading *do not enter, mom*. Nevertheless life for me had finally come together.

One of my many memorable moments was the day I'd inked my first mortgage. The boys and me arrived at our new home, and just after unlocking and opening our front door for the first time, I was forced to stand on the sideline of the hallway to watch them race throughout battling who would get what bedroom. *What a glorious feeling it was.*

Perhaps one would say that my life closely mirrored that of a soccer mom, except I was unmarried and soccer was not exactly the sport that consumed a great deal of my time. Witnessing rebounds and touchdowns had become my responsibility in between chasing a paycheck.

Thankful was an understatement after having accomplished a substantial amount of what my heart desired. There wasn't much more I could ask of my life's present hour. So my prayer to God would always end with an effortless *thank you*. Particularly

A lunch date with my special guy

because at that moment in time, I did not perceive my life as being governed by that of a family curse.

* * *

Veteran homeowners regularly advised me of the benefits of considering a family friendly neighborhood home. So I was thankful for the reputation of our community, except for when residents would slowly bypass my house and poke fun at my version of a manicured yard. It took me some time to realize that the blades of a lawnmower were adjustable, so my yard was often as bald as the palm of my hand.
These critical individuals were considered the retired nosey neighbors.

Although I was not fond of their criticism, I had discovered over time that it was advantageous to reside around their prying, *particularly for a single mother like myself.* My boys, on the other hand, hated this. They despised this to the core because there never existed enough time for them to conjure up *what I considered* the half-truth to their story if ever they were disorderly while outdoors. From one end of our street to the other, and then around some of the neighborhood cul-de-sacs, my phone number was stored in a cellphone, or posted on a refrigerator. And sure enough, I would receive a call if either of them made the decision to two-wheel their way through someone's neatly arranged flowerbeds or use Monday night football voices instead of moderate outdoor expressions while playing street sports.

Contrary to there being advantages to living within close proximity to such neighbors, there existed those disadvantages far more greater than being evaluated for my inability to take pleasure in Martha Stewart's healthy lawn care tips. It was one thing for them to be facetious in that case, but it was another to have them spread whispers throughout the community and be critical of my visitors, *like the time I'd received an unexpected visit from the county sheriff. **I was blinded by liberation.***

Our first home

Psalm 23:4-5
Even though I walk through the valley of the shadow of death, I will fear no evil, for you are with me; your rod and your staff, they comfort me. You prepare a table before me in the presence of my enemies; you anoint my head with oil; my cup overflows.

10

Shutting the Blinds

Gasping for air, it was evident that breathing had suddenly become a struggle. So did maintaining my posture just after ripping open the manila folder only to find legal papers I had received in exchange for that of my signature. Noticing my name as the defendant, I knew that my destiny involved yet another courtroom *and a child.* This time I was being sanctioned for the last one I'd spared my uterus for. My heart quivered as I suffered with a feel of a sharp burning stick jabbing me right in my soul. I felt the urge to pass out across my hardwood floors, but instead I was subjected to experiencing a flashback moment.

(Flashback #1: Day of Delivery)

His heart had stopped just after the rupturing of my membrane. My water had broken. Right after, I perceived that something wasn't right because the nurse aggressively yelled out for the doctor, the MD who'd spent the last nine months preparing me for the opportunity to cuddle my third son for the first time.

"How far is the doctor away?" the nurse begged of the medical professionals who packed my birthing room.

It was obvious she was a skilled health care provider and wanted me to believe that she was calm. That wasn't the case. I could tell that she was a tab bit ruffled and that the matter was urgent. Keeping me calm was her objective, and she was doing her due diligence to accomplish just that. I credit this to her opting to tell me very little of what my very own body and baby experienced. She was not fazed by my consistent inquiry, and was disinterested in increasing my blood pressure just before delivery. Instead, she continued compressing away at my abdomen hoping to retain life for my baby and me. Still his heart failed to pump. The flush from the break of my water frightened him like a bad dream, causing his heart to cease the pumping it had done for nearly forty weeks. All I could do was pray that everything was okay, but even that was a task because of the excruciating contractions. Losing my child would kill me. I questioned if this was God's way of saying I wasn't ready to be a mother for the third time, or was it the perceived curse I felt existed? For nine months, I'd synced lullaby riddles with each of his energetic kicks. I had even spent my four trimesters living in black and white. I was black, and everything in my apartment sheets and all had to be white. I know this may make me seem as if I resided in one of those insane asylums, and I was *okay with one having that notion. Reality was, the simplest of colors had a lasting result of my becoming terribly nauseated. Furthermore, after enduring the agony of living in black and white, I couldn't even depend on those munchies I would crave because they too had a lasting effect. Just after stripping my kitchen down to that one desirable nibble, like magic I would find myself at the neighborhood emergency occupying a seat in the waiting room right next to lacerations and infections because of my excessive craving for pickles that subjected me to severe allergic reactions. I never knew crunchy dills would make an impression on my lips exactly like that of an air pump to a deflated balloon. They were already full enough.*

Finally, the doctor and her ordained hands arrived, and by the grace of God and of course that of the last two remaining centimeters, I was ready to begin pushing my baby through my cervix, then through my stretched vagina, before introducing him to the real world.

(End of Flashback #1)

The outcome of my painstaking delivery was request for custody papers.

There was no one home to soothe me, so I did my best to cuddle my weakened soul and the pain that accompanied it. As I continued to feel the fire from the legal documents blazing through my fingers, I experienced yet a second flashback.

(Flashback #2: My Sick Baby)

He had almost reached what some considered terrible or terrific two. But it frightened me to experience a what if of him not celebrating his milestone. Like the day I had to schedule an emergency visit to the neighborhood pediatrician.

The waiting room was occupied by that of blocks being thrown, coffee and end tables serving as drums or bongos, and loud outbursts of rage. And my baby was a participant. Never mind the fact that the majority of the offspring's were ill, much like he was. The wait to see the doctor extended beyond what little energy my baby had, so he turned to my chess for embracing. And like always, I held him near and dear.

It was in my arms where my baby loss consciousness, just after stacking his last block and whining his way into my arms. And gracefully, I was thankful to have experienced a motherly intuition by deciding to carry him right to the doctor's office after picking him up from the nursery.

His eyes remained opened and had rolled to the back of his head while his mouth developed an abnormal foam which overflowed from his partially opened mouth, down his cheek and onto my arm.

My cry for help seized the uproar of the waiting area, as others were shocked to see my baby's inert form. Some even tried helping as I passed his little body from my arms to the doctor's secure grip.

His convulsion lasted three minutes. Fifteen minutes could have been deadly, and after our experience in the back of an ambulance, which rushed us to nearest emergency, the doctor turned to me and said heartfelt words. **You saved your baby's life.**

(End of Flashback)

Again I will say, saving my son's life earned me custody papers. It also led to foreclosure of our home. ***I'd become blinded by heartache.***

Psalm 23:4-5

Even though I walk through the valley of the shadow of death, I will fear no evil, for you are with me; your rod and your staff, they comfort me. You prepare a table before me in the presence of my enemies; you anoint my head with oil; my cup overflows.

11

Lost and Found

"Mommy, I miss you so much."

Within a percentage of a second of hearing those words, my face was wet with tears. My chapped lips would snag each one before feeding me an unpleasant taste of salted distress. I could never decode Gods plan with losing custody of my son, considering it was his higher power to

Wearing the stress of a loss custody battle during a weekend visit with my son

bless me with the life of a third bundle of joy. *After all, God could do all things.* But why the plot he'd established for my life would snatch away my blessing was beyond me. I thought that I had survived the

climax of the story he had written for me, but surely I was nowhere near the resolution.

I knew my baby was safe, loved, and warm, but I could not grab him and hug him, kiss him, or even admire his smile, as he now lived nearly four hours away. The judge's verdict had converted my life into that of the walking dead. My dark oily skin had become dry and snowy, my eyes were popping out of my head from that of shock, and my normal poise was paralyzed. *All I was missing was my tombstone*. No doubt

Wearing the stress of a custody battle, during a weekend visit with my son

about it, I felt as if the sun was cruel for waking me every sunny morning with that of dire pain. So all I could say was, "I miss you too, baby."

A significant part of my children's life involved separation grief, and I wanted to prove to those who doubted me that the love I had for my three sons was ordinary. I wanted to prove

My first out of state visit to my have lunch with my

that if I had the ability to move heaven and earth, I would. I wanted to prove that I would give my life for my children, any time or any place. This is what made my love ordinary, except I was unable to show others beyond their doubt. *I was robbed of that chance.*

Although not considered unfit, I still lost. Particularly because my lifestyle couldn't compare to that of his fathers, a multi-millionaire with resources *out the you know what*. It was as if my son had a price tag stamped on his forehead, and it was one I could not afford.

Surviving this apocalyptic moment of my life was difficult. *Because of this, I questioned whether or not the outcome of my year-to-year custody battle was that of the family curse I believed existed. The one that had governed my mother, father, grandmother, and great-grandmother.*

I would resent God, and at the same time cry out to him.

"I tried, God, I did. I'm sorry, I'm sorry."

This only meant that I had become emotionally rocky.

I harbored a grudge toward Him only because I felt that He was terribly wrong in believing that I could endure another subpoena to court, *and another loss.* I wanted to believe what others had preached, and that is, God would never give to one more than they can handle. If He were really compassionate, forgiving, and righteous, He would know that my intentions were there and that I was ready to not only repent, but also sacrifice my life and love for my children for the rest of my days. He did give me more than I thought I could handle, therefore I considered those spiritual sayings as words worth less than a penny with a hole in it.

I was annoyed and bitter with Him.

But it wasn't long after my resentment, that I would begin to discern myself as being selfish. That is because I had crumbled away opportunities with parenting my children during the early part of their lives. And perhaps it was because of me that they would suffer the same pain I now endured from being forced by the judge to say goodbye to a fraction of my heart.

I wanted to be strong and wanted to bring back the best of Ericka, but I lost my way.

* * *

Surrendering my walks of life to the devil would have been a weak-kneed recourse to escape the pain endured from losing my son, but even though anxiety provoked an uncomfortable tremble, my knees weren't that weak. I had become handicapped and self-imprisoned, jailing myself within my own skin, and the strength of my legs was necessary in order to escape that of my emotional affliction. *I couldn't eat, and I could barely sleep,* but selling my soul to such act would have only proved that I was a wimp. Nevertheless, being confined within my own skin was beginning to feel rather claustrophobic, and I was not going to stand for that evil curse serving as the demonic guard that held me captive within.

* * *

Not long after the start of my journey towards healing my soul, I unzipped that one unwanted layer of skin, and stepped right out of it. I had come up with what I considered the perfect distraction from suffering with that of a weakened heart.

I was going back to school. And I was going to pursue my desirable career. I wanted to become a teacher, and pursuing a masters degree was going to be my first step towards repaving my life. Finally, I had made a decision, one that I could live with. At least if the outcome was a bombshell, I could only blame myself.

But first, my confession was that I did in fact go down swinging in my custody battle, and suffered with that of a disastrous outcome, one that could have killed me. But I was not at all interested in allowing the judge's decision to entice me to spend my eternal life burning in hell. Therefore I applied for acceptance into a local college.

* * *

My acceptance was denied.
And as one may imagine, my self-esteem sank again, leaving ample space for anxiety to restock the weight of pain, just enough to hamper me.

The fine print of my rejection letter nearly persuaded me into believing that I was a failure and everything touched by me was still turning to stone. Still, I believed that that of a family curse governed my life. And it had finally sucker punched me onto the ropes. The feeling of defeat meant that emotionally I was in trouble.

I had just lost my baby, and then my confidence in my dream of attaining a master's degree and becoming a teacher. The pain I suffered only enticed me to cry myself to sleep each and every night, and imagine that I was being lowered into my own grave.

My grade point average from my undergraduate studies made me look dumb, or shall I say *not smart*. Unintelligent in the eyes of the top dog of admissions, and my inability to plan my future was to blame.

Even still, I could not give up. Making that an option *was no option*. Adding a denial letter to the judge's verdict was not going to lure me closer to the lake of fire.

So instead of accepting my rejection, I put on my big girl panties and made the decision to write a letter of appeal, and asked the school *for just one more consideration*.

December 23, 2010
Dear ▮▮▮▮,
   Although I have received my denial letter, I have not given up on attaining admission to ▮▮▮▮ College. I understand that my GRE/GPA scores did not meet your requirements and I must say that the score I received is an inadequate representation of my educational capability. For apparent reasons I was hopeful for acceptance, but personal purposes included an opportunity to

embrace my college experience and be extremely dedicated and successful as I continue to pursue my career as an educator, something I was unable to do during undergraduate studies. Mr. ▇, because of my denial letter, I felt it necessary to further introduce myself to you and share why acceptance into ▇ College is so important to me.

  Mr. ▇, I survived the terrifying life of a homeless sixteen-year old parent of two children, despite failure being expected from single, teenage girls who become parents. During this period, I was forced to make a decision of separation from my children with hopes of bettering myself. I gave serious thought to giving up. Realizing I wanted more for my children and myself despite being the center of negative attention because of my life being much different from most of my peers, I embraced the challenges of my circumstances, and decided that the despair around me would not crush my hopes and dreams of being successful.

  With only having high school counselors to depend on, I found myself visiting their office constantly in search for direction. Upon my many visits, they were extremely helpful with providing me with information related to government assistance, but never was I approached with college and/or scholarship information as if they'd assumed that because of my parenting responsibility, I lacked interest in continuing education beyond high school. Without many options, I took their advice and applied for aid from the government, and although very appreciative of their efforts, I knew that welfare was going to be a temporary means of survival for my children and me. Concluding that this was not the life for my family, and me I took leadership of my future, and after graduation and on my own, I enrolled into college with my objective being to gain a college degree. I refused to let difficult times rob me of everything I had worked so diligently to achieve. Through it all, I was determined to graduate, and I did.

  I fully understand and respect your decision to deny me admission, but I do hope you will reopen my file to reconsider my candidacy for your program. Additionally, I hope that it will be noticed that I have lived a life of hard won accomplishments despite tough situations. Now that I am much older and can proudly say that my oldest two sons are preparing to go off to college, I expect to work hard and participate in the experiences of graduate school. It is because of my past experiences that I am now determined to excel at ▇ College so that I can continue helping good people who may have found themselves in difficult, even desperate, circumstances. It is my hope to attend your school, which I know have excellent resources to prepare me to become a contributing member of the education profession. Thank you for your help.

Sincerely,
Ericka Williams

My actual letter of appeal written to the college admission office after receiving denial letter

I could have accepted their decision and chose to waddle in even more misery. *But I didn't.*

If the devil wasn't a liar, I was about to make him into one.

Because not long after I had pressed the send button, I received a response and it read, *accepted.*

This time I looked forward to my response letter because I knew that the fine print of my letter would simply provide me the date to pick up my new college identification card. *I was blinded by lack of success.*

Romans 5 3:5

More than that, we rejoice in our sufferings, knowing that suffering produces endurance, and endurance produces character, and character produces hope, and hope does not put us to shame, because God's love has been poured into our hearts through the Holy Spirit who has been given to us.

*My baby and me during
our weekend visit together in Atlanta.
I was committed to my weekend visits.*

12

I *do* when I really *don't*

Wedding days are meant to be special for both bride and groom, *so I have heard.* These are the waking hours most women eagerly awaits. This is her special occasion, the moment she gets to parade a room in a lavish white gown, no matter the season. *It may be that she chose embroidered satin to be her finish of choice or that of lace to add grace to her eye-appeal.* This is the day she possess the most beauty, regardless of the prettiness of noblewomen in the audience. This short-lived occasion is when her hair may be styled with flawless ringlets accented by a pair of spiral curls looping down her face revealed to its entirety just before kissing her groom. Teary-eyed family members who'd come together to congregate her elegance, and that of the striking handsome groom who often showcases a tailor made suit are stunned by their elegance.

Most women fantasize of this day, and even sketch it out as if they have a groom even when there isn't one anywhere in the near future.

My wedding day was sketched out, except it did not go as planned.

I was not permitted the opportunity to be a showoff.

I did not wear a lavish white dress. As a matter of fact, the evening dress I substituted for a wedding gown would have been perfect for my senior prom. My hair was days old, and held in place by that of a flimsy bobby pin that I'd found just beneath my bathroom sink.

I never paraded a room. Instead I awaited the calling of my name to enter into a courtroom before a judge.

My groom did not possess a tailor made suit. Instead, the suit he'd worn had been strutted down a few halls throughout his workday.

My audience was bare, so bare that mom didn't even share this moment with me.

There were no tears *except for my own*. This is because as I said I do, I also said I don't to so many things about my special day, and the groom I shared it with.

And this didn't dawn on me until I had inked my signature on that of a marriage application.

* * *

Our walks of life collided during my darkest moment, right at the pinnacle of my custody battle and my desire to become a teacher. During this time, he had become a valued confidant. *A man who did not judge me because of my circumstances.*

I wasn't his first wife. Nor was I his second. And since three times is commonly known as the charm, no attention was paid to the problems I once considered a promise.

Every single word of the marriage vow uttered was a lie. I boldly stood before Christ and committed marriage perjury. I did not take thee to be my wedded husband. Although I had him I did not want to hold him, especially not until death did us part. Together we committed love fraud by believing that soul mates were what God made of us. Just after kissing my groom, I began to fear my future. I exited the courthouse with who I had convinced myself was meant to be the half to my whole.

The only part of my vowels to come into fruition were that of sickness and health and that is because I ailed in illness as I envisioned what my future would be like after choosing to marry a man to pay back the debts of an IOU (I owe unto).

My marriage was a private affair. It was widely known that I had wedded. Only few knew whom I had swapped vows with. Together we withheld our nuptials. I never changed my last name, and he never wore a wedding band. That was how confident we were in believing that our marriage was doomed to become that of a divorce. He wasn't vulgar. He wasn't malicious, and I never felt that he would jeopardize my life. I loved him, *but was not in love with him*. He loved me, *but was not in love with me*. Despite the many times we'd said those three words to one another, neither of us experienced being shot with the golden bow and arrow that accompanied Cupid, the God of love. *I said I do to pay back an IOU*. Many times I'd heard that it would be to my advantage to love whoever loved me, but I tried that. It did not work. It was evident that God did not ordain this matrimony, and instead it was a convenient opportunity to become a wife.

Just after saying "I Do"

Instead of experiencing that sexual arousal, I would cringe at the sound of our garage door opening, because I knew that the first thing he would do after arriving home from a late working day is press his lips up against mine. I wanted to experience the kind of love that would send me shivering just by the touch of my thigh. Instead, his fingers felt like that of an air conditioner. The chills I felt were cold and discomforting. I wanted to experience the love that would leave me tingly and wet. The only wetness I would ever endure from him was from that of his tongue. After that, I would depend on lubrication. The man I called my husband could never fulfill my love desires. *I said I do to pay back an IOU.*

I owed him, and in a sense may still be in arrears with him today. Although we were not in love with one another, it was he, my confidant, who encouraged my decision to pursue my master's degree in education. He reminded me to not fault myself for seeking a degree in journalism that only mounted to only being a hefty bill. He would provide support to my children and me whenever I'd fallen short. Never did he judge me for making poor decisions as a mother. Instead, he would cheer me on from the sidelines with making my family back whole in one house, *of course until my custody case*. It was my confidant who assured me that there was still value to my life after fighting and losing custody of my third son, the child I'd hoped would give me the opportunity to be the mother I never was to my first two.

In spite of the support, both mentally and physically, we'd come to terms with reality being he was not my life partner, and I was not his.

Perhaps it was that of the family curse I believed accompanied me through my walks of life, enticing the two of us into believing that we would be together until the end of time. *I was blinded by sin.*

---

1 Corinthians 13:6

It does not rejoice at wrongdoing, but rejoices with the truth.

13

Teac...HER

Finally, I'd accomplished my goal of becoming a teacher. And my classroom had become my salvation, *my escape from painful moments brought about from life in general.* It was as if

The beginning of my career as an educator

the front door were that of white out, gliding right over distractions only leaving the ingredients for making my day of teaching and learning productive. No matter the season, my problems were locked away in my car.

In my classroom, I served as the lighthouse, and my responsibility was to provide to my students a ray of light while preparing them for the currents that were sure to add challenges as they set sail into their future.

Aside from providing them the support needed with developing self-expression, it was in my classroom where I would console my students by reminding them that it was okay to be wrong, as long as they learned from it. This was my strategy used to build confidence in them, and in turn, in myself. I even found it necessary to teach the difference of winning and losing and how regardless the outcome what mattered was the effort. Much like my decision to defend myself after receiving a denial letter. I turned a loss into win, and I wanted them to know that they could do the same. The thought of nearly losing the opportunity to be a mentor to them pains me. Despite one's judgment of my character, I proved them wrong.

Within my classroom I would celebrate differences, and judge no one because of their personal circumstances, rich or poor. In room it did not matter.

My classroom was where I stood the moment I'd realized my purpose besides that of my own children. And that was to impact the youth, and not consume myself with the possibilities of there existing a family curse. It was my classroom to distract me from believing that my shadow was my evil twin, which meant striving to overcome internal conflicts. It was my classroom where I would become a leader, and groom others into becoming the same.

Often times, it was my classroom where I would provide a granola bar, a breakfast sandwich, or even a pair of gently worn shoes to students who parents struggled to do the same.

In between lessons, I would silently pray not only for self-deliverance, but for prosperity for all of my students. Standing before them, I would celebrate with excitement or display disappointment when I felt lack of effort.

It was my classroom where I would become known as a school mom, a title I proudly accepted. *It was my classroom and my precious students who brought me so much joy.* **I blinded myself from suffering.**

Romans 12:6-7

We have different gifts, according to the grace given to each of us. If your gift is prophesying, then prophesy in accordance with your faith; if it is serving, then serve; if it is teaching, then teach.

ERICKA N. WILLIAMS

14

Was it a M.A.T.C.H?

I was ready to date, and so I threw a penny in the well after making a wish for that special man. I was ready for a partner. I was ready to be in love. And since I'd caught wind of one success story after another, I took my chances at online dating. After all, it was no longer necessary to shop for a tastefully fitted dress paired with a stylish pump that squeezed at the wideness of my size nine. Technology had brought dating within convenient reach with that of the remote control, a comfortable pajama set, a pair of slippers, and of course a cozy couch. These were the perfect necessities to sending a wink every now and again, with hopes of receiving one back. Before long, I'd received just that along with an email from a man that stimulated my interest enough for me to dive into my closet in search for the perfect outfit I'd hope would make a lasting impression.

* * *

It seemed to be a match.

The very moment we met, we were drawn to one another. I wondered if he would be the man I would spend my days thinking about, and the one I would spend my nights dreaming about. I was curious if he was the one I would share my life with, and the one I would fall in love with, *and who would fall in love with me*. In time, he brought me pure joy, and I strived to deliver to him the same. His presence was all I needed. Any time he would look at me, he would take my breath away. I would just stare at him and smile. The world would stop whenever he would kiss me, and I had hoped to experience them eternally. From experience, I'd learned that a kiss lacks pleasure when it is with someone I didn't have interest in. Certainly that was not the case with him. My lips felt at home against his.

One of my happiest moments in love

Being with him made me feel complete.

And then he told me he loved me, and I told him the same.

For the first time in my life, I felt what it was like to love someone who seemed to be the last of my kind. The kind of person who I wanted to explore and experience with, and the person who I enjoyed doing absolutely nothing with.

We spent quality time speaking love language.
We ran the same course.

I must admit, it was a bit fearful jumping on the bandwagon of love because no one wants to strategically place himself or herself in position to be hurt. But I trusted that he would not cause me to crash and burn.

Our vacation together cruising the coast

A significant part of our relationship was balanced.

He would provide dinner, and I would provide the dessert.

He would pay for the movie, and I would pay for the popcorn.

He would provide the peanut butter to my jelly.

He would provide his hand, and I would provide mine for that moment of prayer.

He was the man I'd captured meaningful memories with.

He wasn't perfect, but he was perfect for me. *He himself agreed that there was nothing that the two of us could not conquer together, and I believed him.*

* * *

As with any relationship, we began facing challenging moments. In spite of the obvious, I remained rooted to my commitment to accepting his good, bad, and his indifferences, because I loved him. And I had prayed to God that he would return to me the very same ingredient for brewing a lasting love. This task for him was a challenge.

Eventually the honeymoon period was over. Instead of teaching me how to love him, and allowing me to teach him how to love me, he chose to treat my heart like that of a revolving door. After all the fun, he'd change.

I was blinded by a dream.

Proverbs 22:24

Do not associate with a man given to anger; Or go with a hot-tempered man.

15

July 13, 2017

It was a routine eye examination that reordered the vital spirits of my life, making this the most taxing day ever lived, ever more barbed than the moment I'd lost custody of my son.

When all was said and done, a reciting of the running letters on a snellen chart ultimately ended with an MRI of my brain, a butt revealing johnny gown, socks with gripping soles, and lack of certainty.

Minutes after receiving the negative outcome of my MRI

The *experienced* optometrist detected something perturbing, a diagnosis she'd only seen during her vision care and eye care studies. My left eye endured very little blood circulation, thereby provoking the color red that I'd caught sight of from that of my right to appear orange from that of my left. Additionally, she'd discovered abnormal festering forming around the one eye that hadn't steered me wrong yet.

My vision was in trouble, and I needed the expertise of a neuro-ophthalmologist, and a neurosurgeon.

The black and white replication of my brain upon the MRI chart clearly revealed a benign tumor, and it was aggressively overpowering my optic nerve by forcing blood to flow away from my eye, and not to it, as it should have.

The last picture I took before brain surgery

And although my right eye proved accuracy, truth was the festering indicated that I was at risk of becoming completely blinded.

In spite of my desire to wake from what I'd hoped was a horrific dream, reality was brain surgery would be the only option I'd have to save my life and *vision*.

Encountering a massive stroke or possible death were my only other options. As I made my decision to go under the knife, there were thoughts of my three sons, my mother and father, and the man who'd stolen my heart. I desired more earthly time with them all, so I laid my life atop the hospital bed and prepared my heart for the medical procedure. If there really existed a family curse, I hoped it had become too busy with taunting other aspects of my life than to accompany me during my perished state from that of the anesthesia.

* * *

My life was spared, and so was the ability to see *out of only my right eye*. From my left eye, it was as if I were asleep when my eye was wide opened. Removal of the tumor left me partially blinded. Vision from my perspective resembled that of a missing headlight on that of a car. This meant that it was very unlikely that I would ever view life the same, I would never see my children the same, and I would never see myself the same. Because of this, I'd fallen victim of *stress response syndrome* and will opt to not add any additional moments of this day to my writing. I had become captive by that of depression. **I had become blinded, literally.**

Psalm 146:8

The Lord opens the eyes of the blind. The Lord lifts up those who are bowed down; the Lord loves the righteous.

16

Desperately Seeking Strength

Every morning, I would wake from a sleepless night only to feel as if I were dead, buried and forgotten by some of those I once considered dear and close to my heart. When reality was they did not give a damn about me.

I would face my emotionless expressions, and struggle with identifying myself. Even felt shame for the outside world to see me. Life for me was much like that of an infant left to experience growth all alone. If I were to compile a list, it would break my heart to see some of the names of those who chose to walk out on me, *even the man I loved unconditionally.* "You're strong enough to handle this, Ericka." He took pride in saying those words to me as he stood at the entrance of my heart, but at the exit of my front door.

The outcome of my brain surgery confirmed to me that depression was real. It was bona fide authentic. And it was vicious just as Michael Myers was on the horror movie

Halloween, or like that of Jason, from Friday the 13th. They were demonic characters, and depression was wicked as it sought out individuals who in most cases were victimized while they were alone. I had become its sufferer.

The first picture I took after brain surgery

Every mirror in my house had to be smothered with a blanket or sheet. A great deal of my head was bald and zipped closed. My dependable eye was nearly swelled shut from the constraint of the surgery. My heart was shattered into miniature pieces. And there existed no confidence. Catching sight of myself only pained me even more as I rebelled against having to look at the stitches stretched from the top of my head, down my temple, ending at the peak of my left ear.

There is no word to explain the sense of loneliness I felt at this time of my life.

I can't say that about the first two weeks of my recovery though. Mom was in town, local aunts and cousins I never see or hear from stopped by, and those I once considered dear friends at one point but hadn't seen in years paid me visit. Day and night shifts were even created. It was during that time I would try my hardest with being strong, as I felt supported. The man I loved would see to it that I was bathed and comfortably tucked away in fresh clean pajamas, and would lie next to me at night. This made me feel loved. But just after my two-week visit to the doctor, things changed.

Some of those very people began to consider me weak, pathetic and in search for attention. Particularly after my mind had been captured by that sorrowful D word. *Even my own children settled on prioritizing other aspects of their life, ranking those things as more important than simply being in my presence or even saying the words I had longed for.* I Love You.

Early mornings and late evenings, I found myself crying out to God in between asking him *why*. These weren't internal cries, either. I spoke out to him, as if he lay on the pillow next to the one I seeped bodily liquids from my head upon. I would feel the urge to read my bible, but couldn't. It was the word I needed, and I was confident in knowing this. But instead I would question my self-worth and my purpose in life if there existed one.

Nevertheless, **I was blinded by self- worth and wanted to die.**

John 10:10

The thief comes only to steal and kill and destroy; I have come that they may have life, and have it to the full.

17

Excuse me as I reminisce…

I thought love had come to me. Despite the pain I'd faced, I spoke to my heart, and asked it to open to the opportunity of loving again. I was afraid and unsure, but I gave in. This time I had felt the yearning I'd longed for. It was as if he looked at me with more than just his captivating eyes. He could even caress me with more than just his manly fingers. His smile, laughter, and presence made me happy. The kind of happy a child often felt on Christmas Eve. I had believed that he was my Prince Charmer, my Jody, and my soul mate. Without doubt, I was convinced he was just what my heart desired, until the ending of our honeymoon period.

He let me down.

The exact moment I had realized that he would not continue to journey through life with me. But still, I loved him.

Eventually, he removed the mask he'd worn to woo me in since we first laid eyes on each other outside of the Internet dating site. Beneath that mask stood a complete stranger. It hurts me to face the veracity of this, but truth is, the man I'd fallen in love with embezzled my heart.

He let me down.

I had fallen in love with a man who lacked empathy and the meaning of unconditional love. I knew that I wasn't perfect, but I also knew that the ingredients of true love involved communication, overcoming relationship issues, commitment, and forgiveness. Looking back over my relationship, I was mostly judged and crucified for my wrong saying and doings, despite my valuable traits. They didn't matter. Such qualities would require removing the training wheels and experiencing real life and real issues. Mature love acquits not die. Immature love does not like demands, and neither did the man who eventually taught me what it felt like to endure bewildered love. Everything was my fault. He was my world, but in time I realized I wasn't his.

He let me down.

In the matter of two years, I'd suffered with the feeling of abandonment. I'd even felt devalued, and discarded all because of my desire for a mature love with him. Unlike the love I had for him, he could only love me when things were passionate, sexy, and romantic; his version of good. God forbid the moments I would be expressive. He made mistakes in our relationship, and I would forgive him because I had always believed that it was the Godly thing to do. When I made mistakes, he would hold a grudge.

It pains me to face the truth that the man I loved with my heart and soul walked out on me for practically anything, treating my heart as that of a revolving door. And I am not exaggerating. I remember for my fortieth birthday, aside from supplying me with passionate love making, he provided me with a break-up as a gift.

Even still I loved him and prayed for change.

It was as if he only engaged in critical thinking, only to find the perfect reason to not love me and make me his wife.

He continued to let me down, and I continued to pray for change.

The only man I had ever utterly loved provided me with dyer pain. I was forgiving of his wrongs, but he could not replicate this back in return.

I was blinded by love ***until literally becoming blinded.***

---

1 Timothy 6:3-5

If anyone teaches a different doctrine and does not agree with the sound words of our Lord Jesus Christ and the teaching that accords with godliness, he is puffed up with conceit and understands nothing. He has an unhealthy craving for controversy and for quarrels about words, which produce envy, dissension, slander, evil suspicions, and constant friction among people who are depraved in

mind and deprived of the truth, imagining that godliness is a means of gain.

18

Empathy or Apathy

"You're too needy."

I will never forget those words *and not because they were music to my ears.* Instead, these were words muttered to me from the man I loved. Words I would have never replicated to him. This was his motive for walking out on me after brain surgery, shutting the door right in my face. I thought it was okay to need a loved one after being sliced with that of a scapel or 10 blade. But the same man who recited to me, over and over again that he loved me was the very man to hammer me regardless of my pain and suffering from a life-saving surgery. *From his perspective, there was no such thing as the right time to face difficult moments.*

As I look back on the nasty words recited to me, I realize that he charmed me just enough to lead me to believe that it was okay to fall in love with him, but only to turn around and provide me distasteful examples of verbal abuse. No matter the situation, I was always wrong.

Before learning that my walk of life included a tumor, and even after the removal of it, when I should have been thinking only of myself, I would ask God to be the strength needed to hold our relationship together.

But even with praying for both he and myself, I was wrong from his perspective, *as he considered my decision to pray over our good and troubled times an act of manipulation.*

But I still loved him, and hoped that what I had experienced would turn out to be a prank like those recited on April Fools Day.

The man I loved had *transformed* into a stranger.

I originally fell in love with Autobots, but now it was Megatron who would attack me no matter what I would say or do. He would find wrong in anything I felt was right, including a midday call to see how his day was going, and to simply say *I love you.*

This time, he loved me just enough to be by my side from the moment I walked into the hospital, until the stitches atop my head were no longer holding my flesh together. And then like that, he was gone again.

As I had done many times over and over again, every time he would leave me, I would pray for his return and take him back the moment he would return, believing that he would change.

* * *

I remember…

On a bright Saturday afternoon, he gave in to me in spite of my pain. I wanted it, needed it, and had to have it. This was my first time since surgery. It was as if I was a virgin.

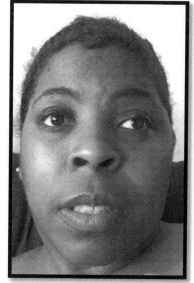
Alone and scared

He pushed it deep inside of me, just after caressing my body with the tongue I had become addicted to. It was like a drug, and I couldn't resist it. Maybe it was because he had become so comfortable with my body. He would outline every part of me with his saliva. I moaned softly, before allowing my cry for more to accelerate to a much louder tune. I loved it, and I loved him. *It was our relationship I was prepared to fight for, no matter what.* I was going to have his back through thick and thin. *Never would I have left his side during afflicted moments.*

The passion was there, and so was the intensity. Our bodies exchanged sweat. His rolling about my double D's, much like a slow flowing river with no currents. And even outlining my lips of passion, as he stroked between my thighs. My eyes rolled to the back of my head, literally. Both the blind eye and the one that witnessed this moment. I began to cry because I knew that at any given moment, he would release himself from inside of me, and fulfill his passion slam in the palm of his hands, just as he'd done a million times before. Watching his hand overflow, slightly dripping about the hardwood floor, excited me. We were synced, in tune. At least, I thought. As he dripped to the floor, I would drip about the bed, allowing myself to lay about a puddle. I didn't want it to end. I wanted to have this moment with him today, tomorrow, and forever more.

It felt like the first time, except it was our last time. Our river had run dry, and there was nothing I could say or do to bring it back a flow. And if I had made an attempt at saying anything, in his eyes it would be a scheme and I would have alternative motives.

I continued to cry. My cry turned into begging, "Please don't give up on us!" I shouted. My pain was evident, both in my heart and between my legs, as he'd become aggressive to what too felt good to him.

"I'm sorry Ericka," he said.

He had given up on our love, and there was nothing I could do about it. Pain was all about me. Inside my spirit, firing through my soul, and ripping at my heart. I was experiencing a hurt that I'd experienced before and hoped to never experience again. My soul was left empty. So empty that I'd become distracted from my own physical pain. Pain of having my head sliced about so that the neurosurgeon could remove the tumor from my brain. At the moment, I wasn't losing one time, I was losing twice. The man I'd loved unconditionally, and the comfort within my own skin. I was forced to manifest from an unimaginable situation, enduring a pain never felt. One involved being dumped, left alone, in shambles by a man who made me fearful of loving him. The other was recovering from removal of the very tumor that robbed me of my vision. The man I had hoped to marry would never stand stern in keeping our relationship secure. I was convinced that I had lived two years **blinded by that of a fairytale love.**

1 Corinthians 13:4-7

Love is patient and kind; love does not envy or boast; it is not arrogant or rude. It does not insist on its own way; it is not irritable or resentful; it does not rejoice at wrongdoing, but rejoices with the truth. Love bears all things, believes all things, hopes all things, endure all things.

19

I Call her *G*Ma

Not all *family* is blood. At times they start as friends, confidants, or workmates. In their role as being a friend though, they usher a sense of loyalty often sought after in authentic bloodline family, but to no avail. I believe this to be true because this is how the relationship between Barbara, my God given godmother, and me emerged. *I call her G Ma.* She and I worked together, and shared a small office that provided us just enough space to discuss business matters, *and to become like family.*

There was a significant difference in our ages, so I often turned to her for advice because I knew that there was no value to her being untruthful to me, no matter the point or issue. After all, she was like a mother to me, *even*

Barbara, my G Ma, at my Masters of Education Graduation in 2013

older than my own mom.

The bond we'd established and took part in was validated during my long drawn out custody battle, and then that of my brain surgery. *She never thought twice about coming to my defense because she knew my heart.*

Aside from dragging me from one doctor's appointment to another, she would allow me to spend many of my gruesome nights, sleeping next to her in her king sized bed, as I would cry myself to sleep, and toss and turn from real live nightmares. And then there were those early morning conversations where she would extend to me a stern voice of confidence, reminding me that I was strong enough to pull through my pain, even when I felt I couldn't go on. She despised having to witness how I'd loss value of my own greatness.

Feeling dead although thankful to be alive

"You've always been strong, Ericka. Don't you dare stop now."

She would reiterate this over breakfast, lunch, and dinner or while she would clean the incision that spread across my head. *No matter the time, she would encourage me to fall back in love with myself.* If she sensed I needed to hear it again, she would make herself available to be the broken record I needed to listen to, over and over and over again.

Barbara depended on the spirit of God with every aspect of her life and would include me in her prayer because she knew that only God could deliver me from the state of mind I suffered.

That's what friends are for, right?

She never shied away from reminding me of the presence of God, and just how he would not leave me, even when those who I thought loved me left me in the dark.

She lived nearly an hour from me without traffic. This didn't stop her from bobbing and weaving her way through traffic to rescue me from my loneliness, which existed roughly ten or fifteen minutes from an actual cousin or aunt, none of which extended a spare bedroom to me, let alone the opportunity to snore in their ear. *I am forever grateful to this woman.* ***I was blinded by false hope.***

Proverbs 27:9

Oil and perfume make the heart glad, and the sweetness of a friend comes from his earnest counsel.

ERICKA N. WILLIAMS

20

The Pill *will* Kill

A fair amount of recovery time took place at my dad's house as well. Between he and Barbara, I was only home alone long enough to suffer from lack of an appetite, toss and turn from the inability to sleep, load and unload my suitcase with pajamas I'd grown exhausted from wearing, and to conjure up a secret plan of self-destruction.

It was one of the late night news features to pose to me a proposition.

Health officials were surrounding an alarm on opioids, a legal pain reliever that included heroin, an illegal substance considered extremely addictive and life threatening. It was also a prescription that sat next to my bedside, prescribed to ease my pain and suffering. I must confess, *now that I am at a much healthier state of mind, I must be honest in saying that the local news is probably not the best screen saver while one battles with that D word.*

My low spirits began to retaliate against my desire to be optimistic about a brighter outlook. During this time I had begun to feel sorry for myself evermore. So I turned my attention from that of the depressing news to the bottle that was filled to the childproof rim with a definite outcome of overdosing.

I remained hypnotized by the capsules, unable to blink. My bedroom appeared like that of the twilight zone.

Not long after, I'd made sure to include this substance in my suitcase as I prepared to spend days at my daddy's house. I was ready to use it to ease my discomfort-in a way that I would never endure pain again, and my desired results would only come to fruition by choosing to not follow the order as it read on the pill bottle- *do not exceed the prescribed daily dosage.*

At daddy's house in an unrecognizable state of mind. My spirit had been taken over by that of evil thoughts.

* * *

Timing was perfect. Daddy was asleep, and it was just my pills, and me *or maybe even the family curse,* which awaited my decision to press down on and twist off the childproof lid. The decision to destroy myself could have been a quick undertaking. All I needed to do was pour the poison into my dry mouth, and sprinkle some water within my throat. And just like that, the outcome experienced by others who'd overdosed could also be my destiny. At least at that point, I would no longer suffer the pain of being a victim of a broken family. I wouldn't have experienced what it was like to hurt my children, or even endure the pain from losing my youngest from a custody battle. I wouldn't have to be emotionally abused by the man I'd hoped to spend the rest of my life with, and the man I'd just said I love you to over and over again, and meant it.

As a matter of fact, just hours before I sat in privacy, me and my pills prescribed by the doctor, I suffered another raging phone call where my character was degraded, as he tried to convince me of my being wrong, for only God knows what. Never did he ask how I was doing. He cared less of my pain. He had a point to make, and damn he was going to make it right then, regardless of my troubled time.

I was hurting and felt that I wanted to die.

Dying meant no longer being judged, when I only desired to be loved. And for crying out loud, dying meant not having to live with being blinded in one eye.

But then it dawned on me.

I was portraying myself as being a weak woman, a trait Barbara reminded me was by far not the Ericka she'd grown to know and love. *I was also being selfish.* My greatest fear was to ever have to bury my children, so how dare I appoint my own mother to having to cite *ashes to ashes and dust to dust* over my lifeless body. And then there were my children, who would suffer for the rest of their lives from my decision *to choose* to take my last breath. I even wondered…would I be found innocent or guilty from God Almighty. I knew that suicide was sinful, but in all my days I wondered if God really existed. And if he had, why is it he caused me to face a great deal of suffering.

Essentially I did not want to die.

I only wanted the pain to go away. Killing myself also ran the risk of killing those I knew loved me. I'd heard that only faint-hearted people would take their own life. Faint-hearted was not one of my traits. And instead of viewing myself as such, I'd come to realize that not only was suicide real, but it could only defeat those who would allow it to. I realized that taking my own life would not end the chances of life getting worse, particularly for my children. Committing such act only eliminated me from the possibility of ever experiencing what it was like for life to get better.

So instead of convincing myself to cause an explosion to my heart, literally from that of the opioid, I'd realized that God had just given me all the reasons I needed to face the battle he'd bestowed upon me, only because he knew that I was strong enough to fight back.

My life was like that of a broken puzzle, and the one piece I'd felt was missing was God.

My heart was pained. My life was either moments from ending, or beginning. I chose the latter. All of my life, I've had to fight. I am not stopping now. So I chose to cradle my fears.

Was I depressed? Yes. But truth was, I feared that of hell and eternal damnation. And regardless of my own pain and suffering, I loved my children, my mother, my father, my students… and the man who had hurt me. Despite it all, I chose to forgive and that is because God had made his presence known, confirming that he was real and forgiving was the Godly thing to do.

So I chose to put the pill bottle down. And then I chose to drag myself out of the bed before standing before a nearby mirror. At that moment, I came to realize that no matter how others viewed me, I viewed myself differently. Despite my loss of vision, I saw beautiful brown eyes. I saw an incision across my head, now considered that of a warrior womb. I no longer saw the ugly duckling. Staring back at me was that of a beautiful white swan. And dammit, I saw a child of God who was worth the fight. Even if it meant standing alone.

At that moment, I chose to go to sleep to only awaken to the smell of bacon, grits, and a sweet aroma of life-*me and my crippled vision.* ***I was blinded by a broken-heart.***

Psalm 34:18-19
The LORD is close to the brokenhearted and saves those who are crushed in spirit. The righteous person may have many troubles, but the LORD delivers him from them all.

21

Recovery is a Craft

A visit to my therapist

I had always believed that if I took one step *God would take two*. His one step was a reminder that trusting man was not the solution to my recovery. I had to trust him- *the higher power that never left me, when others did.* And so I slid my mind body and soul out of my pajamas and replaced my house slippers with that of running shoes, and sprinted my way into a brown leather chair positioned before a psychiatrist. *At first I wondered if the decision to seek help would mean that I was crazed. But I answered my own question, concluding that being crazy meant not seeking help knowing I needed it.* My preconceived opinion of what I once called a shrink was that one would have to live a life of suffering with schizophrenia, or massive diagnose of craziness that would require hypnosis from some pocket clock, as a form of psychological treatment.

Although I had not been mentally diagnosed as being unstable, I had become insanely out of my mind and needed help.

My very first visit taught me more than what I'd imagined. First being that what I was feeling after experiencing a life changing surgery, along with all that I'd gone through, was common. After all, a man who walked in the flesh and wore a white coat had fondled beneath my brain as if he held silly puddy in the palm of his hand. And I had to live with the consequences of it.

My session also revealed truth being that even psychiatrists are in need of a colleague whenever they'd endure painful moments. They weren't excluded.

Because I am a visual learner, I had to craft a mental picture of what I had come to terms with during my pursuit for help.

Well, I chose to compare the obstacles of life as that as a staircase, with each step demonstrating a different drawback from life. And after suffering from that one difficult situation, I would only take

A visit to my therapist

another step upward only to find that that step too would at some point become problematic. In spite of that, I would continue to step upward to only find myself at the very top of my mental staircase. *The pinnacle of decision-making.* Do I give up and jump, or do I turn around and pound the hell out of those same stairs that took me higher emotionally.

I had positioned myself to jump, but realized that that was not my desire, so I chose to stomp my way back to stability, with only God by my side.

James 4:8
Come near to God and he will come near to you. Wash your hands, you sinners, and purify your hearts, you double-minded.

22

The Devil is a Lie

Hell no, my life is not governed by that of a family curse. And if at some point it was, I have kicked its ass.

Through it all, I am still breathing, walking, talking and experiencing life as God has planned. *Regardless of my vision loss.* Most importantly, I am still smiling. It took standing alone to realize my self-worth, my power, and my ability to fight back.

Many people have wasted life's precious time judging others, including myself. I have judged and been judged. The greatest pain though is being judged by those you love.

My grandmother was judged, but had a heart of gold. Her treks of life did not permit her the opportunity to prove this to the world. Those she loved judged her. And as she rests in peace, I have committed my remaining days to embracing her beauty…the part of her many failed to catch glimpse of because of becoming blinded by that of her liquor bottle. We shared very little time together, but I want the world to know that I love my grandmother, and I am proud of her for fighting her pains as best as she knew how. And who knows, maybe she and Jody are now *dancing* to their favorite blues music, instead of sitting on a filthy porch.

My mother was judged, but she proved to be a warrior. Yes, she experienced life of substance abusing, and even fear of overdosing from one hit too many. But through it all, as she attended funerals of those she once experienced getting high with, God was healing her from her addiction. For years my mother was regarded as the black sheep, but regardless of how others perceived the life she once lived, she is heroic. *Most importantly, she is my hero.* It's been over twenty-five years since my mother took a hit. As a matter of fact, her desire for drugs was replaced with that of a loving husband, and a son who makes her happy. Christian, my brother brings mommy much joy…but me on the hand, *a headache.* ☺ William, my stepfather brings my mother pure happiness, and for that I am thankful. If ever she had met Anthony, her brother, I believe my mom's life would be perfect. Drugs and alcohol could have wiped her off of the face of the earth, but God had another plan for her. The life she has always desired has come into fruition, excluding that of drugs and alcohol. *She won't even take one sip,* therefore I will never have the opportunity to experience Sybil again. *Even still, I believe Hollywood missed out on one hell of an actress.*

Many judged my father. And although it took years for our paths to cross, I have chosen to embrace him as if he was always there. Yes, the streets could have made my father into a victim of crime, but he too was delivered. No more drugs, no more jail time. Nope, I did not have my father for a great deal of my life. But God saw to it that he partook in my life when I needed him the most. My daddy was my friend, my caretaker, and the man who loved me unconditionally while at my weakest. He did not judge me. He simply stood by my side and reminded me of just how beautiful I was, even when I felt that my physical appearance was alienated from that of brain surgery. My daddy assured me that in time, a man would love me unconditionally, as he does, and not judge me for simply being human. My father replaced his life as a street thug with that of being a business owner and husband of many years to Renita, my wonderful stepmother.

I want the world to know that I am thankful to have both my parents, *and that the devil is a lie.*

I have been judged. There exist no person on this earth that has never endured a moment of hardship. But as humans walking in the flesh, they consider themselves as arbitrators of the hardships of others. I made mistakes in my life, and I belittled myself when others penalized me for being *me*. I played down my personal strengths because others wanted to bring light to my moments of darkness. My family judged me, my children judged me, the "judge" judged me, the fathers of my children judged me, colleges judged me, and the man I had hoped to marry judged me. But just when I thought I'd lost everything, I realized that I had found God. Through his revelation, I have come to realize the feeling of being loved. God has been my mother, father, friend, forgiver, protector, and has proven his unconditional love for me. He reminded me of my strengths while cleansing my spirit from that of fraudulent love. He has always proven to be a friend I could depend on. I could tell my problems to him, and he was there to pull me through the rough times, hard times, and trying times. He did not judge me.

The devil is a lie.

John 10:10
The thief cometh not, but for to steal, and to kill, and to destroy: I am come that they might have life, and that they might have it more abundantly.

A Moment of Truth

Emotional pain has a purpose. It's meant to coach one away from unhealthy patterns and relationships. I had been tucking away pain for as long as I can remember, distracting myself from it by any means. This only allowed it to traumatize my mind. Choosing to withhold the pain only decayed my ability to have a clearer focus on life.

After coming to terms with truth being I really did not want to harm myself, I welcomed that of what ailed at me as if it were a friend. That meant welcoming what I felt was a family curse. It was time that I'd come face to face with what I felt taunted those I love and myself. Of course I grew weaker the moment I'd made the decision to fight back. But I convinced myself that just after facing my conflicts, choosing to live without them, I would grow stronger. I would conquer.

Overtime I'd become bruised from those conflicts demanding my attention. But after turning to God, I recognized that in order to win, I had to lose. And I lost a lot, including my perspective to believe that that of a family curse governed my life. This is when I chose to exhale fear and inhale faith. It was God who was there all along.

What I lost
in order to win a relationship with God

Vision in one eye	Time with my children	The man I loved unconditionally and hoped to marry	Confidence in myself
A house made into a home	Friends that were foes	Time with aunts and cousins who were never there	The motivation to go on
Time with my grandmother	Time with my father	Custody of my son	Focus
Time with an uncle I never met	Love for myself	The perspective that God wasn't there	A moment of happiness

Introducing a Stronger and Wiser *Me*
Even When Forced to Stand Alone

ERICKA N. WILLIAMS

Obituary of Dead Words

At one point in my life, I have allowed what others have said to or about me to impact me emotionally. Realizing that they too walk in the flesh and certainly suffer in their own ways, never again will I allow myself to be disoriented. Now that I am stronger and wiser, I will only embrace those who love me for who I am, *not those who judge*.

You are too needy	You're too sensitive	You are insecure	You're a black sheep's child
There exist a family curse	You will never be anything	I love you, but I am not in love with you	You are weak
You're too sensitive	You are weak	You are a failure	You're crazy
You can't	You won't	You will never	You can never find the grey area

Dear Reader,

My decision to share my story was to become someone I once needed when I was younger. The withheld occurrences of my life ultimately became the most powerful parts of my testimony. I was once ashamed, but then I had realized that everyone has a past, but not everyone is emotionally equipped to embrace the shortcomings of their life. Behind my smile was a woman considered strong by most, yet overwhelmed by struggles, although choosing to be resilient as best as one could. I kept walking through every pain and hurt.

Life has taught me that those who are weak seek revenge, those who are strong forgive, those with intelligence ignore. Because I am strong, I have chosen to forgive myself, and those who have wronged me. Because I am intelligent, I have chosen to ignore those who desire to referee my life. *Never will I seek revenge.* I will not be defined by my moments of weaknesses or fear, but by my ability to remain forceful. It took writing my story to face my past so that it does not control my future.

No, my life is not governed by a family curse. God governs it. And this will be my perspective for my remaining days.

Ericka Williams

James 1:2-4

Consider it pure joy, my brothers and sisters, whenever you face trials of many kinds, because you know that the testing of your faith produces perseverance. Let perseverance finish its work so that you may be mature and complete, not lacking anything.

Forever Letters

My Moment of Sincerity

My Definition of a Forever Letter

When I think of the term *forever letter*, I think of writing from an authentic place in my heart. It may be from that of wisdom, appreciation, love, or for forgiving or forgiveness. In order to flush my soul of the pain I have carried all of my life, my forever letters will be written with fortitude and that of emotional presence. My decision to do this will not only grant me the opportunity to better know myself, but also to connect deeply with the letter's recipient, particularly those who have impacted my life.

Thank you for allowing me to publically share my forever letters.

Yours Truly,

Ericka

ERICKA N. WILLIAMS

Forever Letter #1
To My Beautiful Mother

Mommy,

When I think of the beauty of life, I think of you. You are the melodious song from a bird. You are the pure joy I feel from that of children's laughter. You are a breeze on a hot day. You are the smile from that of a stranger. You are the stars in the night sky. You excite me just as much as a new day and that of a good conversation.

An outing with my mom in 2017, at Santa Monica Beach

I want to share with the world how beautiful you are, and how so amazingly proud I am of you. Furthermore, how much I love you.

Ever since I was a little girl, you were my hero. Regardless to how hard life, you made a way for us.

Throughout my life, I discreetly asked God to deliver you from the wicked poison I thought would kill you. He answered my prayer. Not everyone is strong enough to reject what once felt good to him or her, but you did mommy. And given our past, I am so overjoyed that God healed you.

Throughout my life, I prayed that you would someday be blessed with the family you have always wanted and deserved. He answered my prayer. My heart smiles whenever I witness your happiness.

Thank you for showing me grace when I didn't deserve it.

Thank you for comforting me through heartbreaks.

Thank you for your unconditional love and friendship.

Thank you for forgiving me for my mistakes.

Thank you for being strong during tough times.

Thank you for the sacrifices you made in order to make me strong enough to face the world.

At times God would hear my cry for a best friend. He answered my prayer. All along, it was you. Mommy, I want the world to know how thankful I am for your life lessons experienced both directly and indirectly. You are and will always be my hero. Lastly mommy, I want to tell you how sorry I am for the times I let you down, or rebelled against you. When I think of you mommy, I think of the purest love I will ever know.

Proverbs 22:6 Train up a child in the way he should go; even when he is old he will not depart from it.

Forever Letter #2
To My Three Wonderful Sons.

Dear Shawn and Mario,

As a teen mother, I made mistakes. Unfortunately, my mistakes included you. And for that I say, "I'm terribly sorry." I am so thankful that my ability to fight through friction brought you back home to me, providing me the opportunity to be the mother I was once afraid to be.

courtesy of Georgia Southern University

Months before my son's high school graduation,

As I reflect back on your days in middle and high school, I can't help but chuckle at how annoyed you would become because I spent so much time at your school. Well, aside from wanting to be in your presence, I felt the urge to prove to you that I was dedicated to my responsibilities as a mother. It

Quality time with my son

brought me pure joy being a part of your primary years, as I at one point thought that I would never have that chance. I often thank God for bringing our lives back together. And I hope you will forgive me for simply not knowing any better.

Despite it all, I want the world to know that I am extremely proud of the men you have become. And regardless what paths we have journeyed through life, there is no one on the face of this earth that loves you more than I do. *Believe that.*

My son before his fraternity probate

Denim,

You are the wind beneath my wings. I can't define the love I have for you, as no word exists. Even after losing everything including you, you still loved me. You still believed in my unconditional love, in spite of our distance from one another. I cherish the moments you would send me daily bible verses, which confirmed that within you God lived. I thank you for being strong for me when I was weak. My heart trembles whenever I think about the moment you and I had a mommy son talk about my vision loss. You looked at me and said, "Mommy, so what you loss vision. I still have you, and you are still beautiful." I will forever cherish your sincerity for me. There are so many passionate moments we have shared. Like the day you said to me, "Mommy this year for Christmas, I want my gift from daddy to be to help you buy the house you want. I don't want anything else." These heartfelt moments only reminded me that no matter our distance, there is no bond stronger. Mommy loves you always and forever.

My life

Philippians 4:19

And my God will supply every need of yours according to his riches in glory in Christ Jesus.

Quality time in the park with my baby

My baby, safe in my arms

He brings me so much joy

He brings me so much joy

Forever Letter #3
To My Wonderful Daddy

Daddy,

I may remember very little of my childhood, but I recollect the day I laid eyes on you for the first time.

Daddy and Me

And although at that time, I never thought you would be in my life, it was love at first sight.

Ever since then, I never stopped loving you. I only prayed that

Three generations

God would bring you back, and allow me to grow closer to you. He did just that. Daddy, I love you. And I thank you for coming to find me as a child, and embracing me as an adult. The bond we share is never to be broken ever again. My prayer is that through my novel, I am able to convince others to forgive parents who may have made poor choices at parenting. With my decision to ask my own children to forgive me for my mistakes as a teen mom, I realize I must forgive you. There is no difference. And since I fear judgment day, I will never hold a grudge against you for being preoccupied while I desired your presence. I will always honor, regardless.

Daddy, I love and appreciate you.

Ephesians 6:1-3

Children, obey your parents in the Lord, for this is right. "Honor your father and mother" (this is the first commandment with a promise), "that it may go well with you and that you may live long in the land."

Forever Letter #4

To my sister, Nicole

Nicole,

For the first time in my life, I experienced what it was like to have someone drop his or her entire life just to be there for me. That is exactly what you did before and after my surgery. And for that I thank you. At the crack of dawn, you would drag your children out of the comfort of their own bed, just to sleep on my couch as you nursed me back to wellness.

With my little sister, Nicole

I remember the days I felt I could not fight the battle. You looked me in the eyes and assured me that I could, and I want the world to know how much I love and appreciate you for everything.

Over the years, we have established a special closeness, and our bond will forever be cherished. Yes, I am your big sister, and can be a tad bit annoying, but sis I got your back through thick and thin. I love you.

I want the world to know that I thank you for being the person I can go to for anything. Thank you for letting me hug you for no reason. I will forever cherish those moments when we confide in one another. You may be my little sister, but forever are you my friend.

She calls me annoying. I call her my

Forever Letter #5
To the man I loved unconditionally

When I first embarked on day one of our journey, I never envisioned there being an ending. I only considered every day a new beginning for you and I. Our relationship excited me, and I wanted it to last forever. And was ready to attack any opposing force against us.

I have always heard that whenever people walked out on you, never try to convince them to stay. Instead, simply let them go. This was not my desire. I was willing to fight for us. I loved you, and was in love with. I never felt that I had enough hours in the night to hold you, or for you to hold me. But regardless to my feelings, you left me drowning in tears. You were the air I breathed, before being the one to break my heart. I hate the thought of never having the opportunity to sing another love song with you. Instead I must face the truth being that you lead me to walking into a dead end.

Thank you for showing me what it felt like to fall in love. My feelings for you were so sincere, I looked forward to the day that you would need me, only so that I can prove to you that I would uplift you through any and everything life brought your way. For example, if you would have had brain surgery, I would have never left you. How great it would have been to experience the same. How great it would have been for you to want me to love you, instead of convincing yourself that I loved you too much. How great it would have been if only you would have embraced my greatness instead of that of my weaknesses. Whenever I would go to sleep, I would be fearful that when I would awake, you wouldn't be there, only because you continued to leave.

No matter what trial, I believed in forgiving, and I believed in loving. You turned your back on me during my moments of happiness, transforming them into moments of sadness. And then during my weaker moments, you frowned upon my needing you. You even prided saying hurtful things. You saw no value in safeguarding our relationship. You held my hand long enough for me to fall in love, and then you let it go. If I had my way, what we had would have never died. And instead, we would write a best selling love story. Through it all, I want the world to know that I forgive you, and even though you are no longer here, our good memories still linger. And instead of focusing my attention on how you caused me pain, I will embrace those beautiful times we had, and forgive you as I say I love you one more time before wishing you well. I will continue to strive to be the caterpillar that will develop into a beautiful butterfly. God Bless.

One more thing...

This is not manipulation. This is only my way of forgiving you.

Not forgiving will only keep one stuck, and my desire is to be free, ...not angry, even if it means facing reality of you turning your back on us.

I Corinthians 13:4-8

Love suffers long *and* is kind; love does not envy; love does not parade itself, is not puffed up; does not behave rudely, does not seek its own, is not provoked, thinks no evil; does not rejoice in iniquity, but rejoices in the truth; bears all things, believes all things, hopes all things, endures all things. Love never fails. But

whether *there are* prophecies, they will fail;
whether *there are* tongues, they will cease;
whether *there is* knowledge, it will vanish away.

I would also like to extend my heart to ...

Michael Eagan, My Godfather
My Sisters and Brothers:
Christian, Kirsten, Kenyon, Carlos, and Vanity
Barbara Wells
Linda N'zi
If I missed anyone, please charge it to my head, and not my heart.

A Special Thank You to the Beautiful Ladies of Sigma Gamma Rho Sorority, Incorporated

When I think of my life, I am reminded of the beauty of paying it forward. For many years it was my belief that others were meant to learn lessons from the obstacles of my life. This is why God relied on me to maintain strength, one barrier after another.

This photo was taken in the back of a rideshare, on the way to an informational meeting.

After brain surgery in July 2017, I know longer felt that I possessed the strength he once fostered in me. The perspective of my life had turned worthless, and I needed help with redirecting my focus before selling my soul to that of failure. God sent me the sisterhood of Sigma Gamma Rho Sorority, Incorporated. I will never forget…

August 20th 2017, as I lay in the bed, I asked God why must he continue to wake me, forcing me to rekindle with the misery I felt every morning my eyes would open, especially when only one would expose me to freedom. Brain surgery had robbed me of some of my vision, leaving me partially blind. Being at my happiest had to be when I was asleep, therefore my prayer every night was for him to let me rest in peace. After all, there was nothing more he could use me for now that I was partially blinded, having endured a major surgery that could have cost me my life, and my children their mother. Nevertheless, I had grown overwhelmingly exhausted with one door closing on me right after another. This was not the case with SGRHO.

August 24th 2017, your sisterhood, now my sisterhood, opened a door for me, which turned my focus away from being my own villain. It was just four weeks after surgery, and I was invited to learn about an amazing organization, founded by seven beautiful educators, as I too dedicated my life to encouraging educational success to the youth, as a teacher. Despite my impaired vision, and my fragile being, the email sparked my interest, and struck me with many questions, one being was it God answering my prayer, by possibly opening a door for me, proving that when one door closes, another open. I had to see for myself so…

I followed the requirements of dressing professionally, using what little strength I possessed to at least figure out how I could incorporate a head wrap in my professional attire in hopes of covering an awfully wide incision across my head. I could not drive, so I must thank God for rideshare businesses. As I hopped in the backseat of a reliable drivers car, with little vision, I didn't know that my sixty dollar round trip ride would be worth every penny, and then some. It was that ride that changed my life, introducing me to being a part of something far greater than I'd imagined.

Why must I pay it forward? Well, because had you not believed in me, distracting me from the dangers of my very own thoughts, I am afraid to imagine the possible outcome of my self-impression. Some woman has experienced some segment of my life, and too may have asked God to save them from their own self. It is with my beautiful sisters of Sigma Gamma Rho Sorority, Incorporated that I cast the shame of my life to the side, exposing them to learning opportunities for others, as I now pledge to be a servant of God, and that of SGRHO. Thank you for believing in me. EE-YIP.

Signed,

Soror Ericka Williams

Thank you for allowing me to reveal private pains I have endured throughout my life. Each chapter was written from my heart, and exposes what I once considered hush-hush. Not everyone is woman or man enough to let it all out. That no longer involves me. Despite loss of vision, I have a far greater outlook on life and the parts of it I desire to interact with. It is my belief that God saves the best for last, so maybe that's why I remain at the end of the line.

From this day forward, the blueprint of my life will involve lesser judging and more loving. This also means that I will take one step after another in the direction away from those who judge me, only to leave room for those who love Ericka for who she is…not who they want me to be.

It's amazing how much lighter I feel, now that I have released excessive weight. *And to think*, I didn't bust a single sweat or hyperventilate from over doing it on some treadmill or something. My workout is not done though. My prayer is that my transparency and dedication to the life God has for me will motivate others to come face-to-face with heart wrenching life experiences that have held them captive. For the rest of my life, I will not be making sense to please others. Instead I will be making faith, which is a no judge territory. It feels good to now know that my future is far greater than my past, and that is because **only stars shine in the darkness.**

Now, if you would excuse me. *I think I see another blessing whirling in my direction.* ☺

Colossians 1:17

He is before all things, and in him all things hold together.

This is not the end...

This is the beginning.

Made in the USA
Columbia, SC
11 June 2018